SPIRIT & LIFE

SPIRIT & LIFE

— ESSAYS ON —

INTERPRETING THE BIBLE
IN ORDINARY TIME

EMMAUS
ROAD
PUBLISHING

Steubenville, Ohio
A Division of Catholics United for the Faith

SCOTT HAHN

Emmaus Road Publishing
827 North Fourth Street
Steubenville, Ohio 43952

Library of Congress Control Number: 2009920748
ISBN: 9781931018531

Cover design and layout by
Theresa Westling

Cover artwork:
Werner Forman / Art Resource, NY
An illumination from a Byzantine manuscript depicting St Matthew.

Contents

Preface

Several years ago, with friends and colleagues, I founded the St. Paul Center for Biblical Theology. The Center's mission is two-fold: to promote biblical literacy for Catholic laity and biblical fluency for clergy and teachers. Our programs, correspondingly, fall into two categories: our "Letter & Spirit" programs and our "Breaking the Bread" programs. The first group—including our scholarly journal and academic conferences, as well as our monograph series—serves scholars, clergy, and catechists. The second group—including our radio outreach and abundant Bible-study resources (online and on paper)—serves ordinary folks in the parish.

Our work falls into two categories. But there is also a certain unity to the mission. We want to meet people where they are, but we want to stretch them, too. We want ordinary lay Catholics to develop a deep hunger for biblical wisdom—for theology. We want Catholic clergy and teachers to burn with a desire to communicate God's Word simply and clearly, for universal understanding.

We want biblical interpretation to be not just the province of academic specialists—though we need them, too—but also the ordinary stuff of the ordinary life of the ordinary Catholics in ordinary time.

This book is representative of our mission. It's a collection of my essays and addresses on biblical themes. Some of the chapters were composed for lay audiences. Some were composed for teachers and scholars. In all cases, I tried to let myself be stretched by the task and stretched by God's grace. In all cases, I asked God to give me words that would do the same for my readers and listeners. I hope they stretch you, too, whether you're a scholar or you're just undertaking your first serious Bible study.

Scripture was canonized for all of us, all the Church. And it's my dream to see a new generation learn how to "read the Bible from the heart of the Church."

Now, that phrase can have many meanings, all of them true. It suggests the dispositions we should have when we approach the Scriptures. We are trusting children of God and of the Church, our mother. We read the sacred page within a community that's larger than our local Bible-study group or our university's department of theology. Our "study group" is the communion of saints, the voices of Tradition, the great cloud of witnesses from all of history. Our guide is the Holy Spirit, working through the Church's Magisterium.

My colleagues and I mean all this when we urge people to "read the Bible from the heart of the Church."

But, most importantly, we mean that Catholics should read the Bible in its natural and supernatural habitat. We should read the Bible in light of the liturgy.

The Bible and the liturgy were made for one another. That statement would have seemed self-evident to the apostles and the Church Fathers. There were no printing presses in their day, and very few people could afford to have books copied out by hand. So people did not so much read the Scriptures as absorb them, mostly in the Mass. The Mass itself is a stunning compendium of scriptural texts, and it has always included extended readings from both testaments.

In the early Church, the Bible was considered a liturgical book. Indeed, the canon, the official "list" of books in the Bible, was originally drawn up to limit the texts that could be used as readings in the Mass.

But the connection goes back even further than that. For the scriptural texts themselves presume the context of the Mass. The apostles and evangelists seem to be writing with liturgical proclamation in mind.

If we read the Bible as they wrote it, we'll read it from the heart of the Church. And that heart is Eucharistic. It is the heart of Jesus.

The Pontifical Biblical Commission put it well in its 1993 document *The Interpretation of the Bible in the Church*: "It is above all through the liturgy that Christians come into contact with Scripture. . . . In principle, the liturgy, and especially the sacramental liturgy, the high point of which is the eucharistic celebration, brings about the most perfect actualization of the biblical texts. . . . Christ is then 'present in his word, because it is he himself who speaks when Sacred Scripture is read in the Church' (*Sacrosanctum Concilium*, no. 7). Written text thus becomes living word."

That last line packs a lot of punch. "Written text thus becomes living word." It can stand as the motto for this book. Though it refers to the liturgy, it could also serve as a motto for college courses in Scripture and theology. It should set a high standard for any home or parish Bible discussion.

When it comes to Scripture study, the Church has set a challenging agenda for all of us. And no one is exempt. It's not just for priests. Not just for scholars. The Word was incarnate and inspired for you and for me.

Put in those terms, it should be clear to us: biblical literacy is an expression of love; so is biblical fluency. It's reading the Bible from the heart.

Abbreviations

Old Testament

Gen./Genesis
Ex./Exodus
Lev./Leviticus
Num./Numbers
Deut./Deuteronomy
Josh./Joshua
Judg./Judges
Ruth/Ruth
1 Sam./1 Samuel
2 Sam./2 Samuel
1 Kings/1 Kings
2 Kings/2 Kings
1 Chron./1 Chronicles
2 Chron./2 Chronicles
Ezra/Ezra
Neh./Nehemiah
Tob./Tobit
Jud./Judith
Esther/Esther
Job/Job
Ps./Psalms
Prov./Proverbs
Eccles./Ecclesiastes
Song/Song of Solomon
Wis./Wisdom
Sir./Sirach (Ecclesiasticus)
Is./Isaiah
Jer./Jeremiah
Lam./Lamentations
Bar./Baruch

Ezek./Ezekiel
Dan./Daniel
Hos./Hosea
Joel/Joel
Amos/Amos
Obad./Obadiah
Jon./Jonah
Mic./Micah
Nahum/Nahum
Hab./Habakkuk
Zeph./Zephaniah
Hag./Haggai
Zech./Zechariah
Mal./Malachi
1 Mac./1 Maccabees
2 Mac./2 Maccabees

New Testament

Mt./Matthew
Mk./Mark
Lk./Luke
Jn./John
Acts/Acts of the Apostles
Rom./Romans
1 Cor./1 Corinthians
2 Cor./2 Corinthians
Gal./Galatians
Eph./Ephesians
Phil./Philippians
Col./Colossians
1 Thess./1 Thessalonians

2 Thess./2 Thessalonians
1 Tim./1 Timothy
2 Tim./2 Timothy
Tit./Titus
Philem./Philemon
Heb./Hebrews
Jas./James
1 Pet./1 Peter

2 Pet./2 Peter
1 Jn./1 John
2 Jn./2 John
3 Jn./3 John
Jude/Jude
Rev./Revelation
(Apocalypse)

Spirit

Sacred Scripture must be read and interpreted in the light of the same Spirit by whom it was written.

—Dei Verbum, no. 12

Chapter One

The Word of God as a Symphony

What's the Word?

You and I might answer that question in many different ways, depending on the context in which it's asked. "The word" could mean the latest news ("The word on the street is …"). Or it could mean a decisive command ("The word from the corner office is …"). Or it could simply mean a word—a basic unit of language, like the little clusters of the alphabet that make up this sentence.

There are many definitions of "the word," and we don't reduce them much if we clarify the phrase by speaking of "The Word of God." In religious language, and even in the Bible, "The Word" can mean many things. It can involve, for example, a simple sacred upgrade of the definitions I already mentioned—as when "the word of the Lord" means news that comes to a prophet (see Ez 15:1) or when something happens by the command of "the word of God" (see Ps. 33:6–9, Is. 55:11).

In popular preaching in the United States, the phrase usually means one or both of the following: the *written* Word of God—that is, the Bible—or the incarnate Word of God—Jesus Christ.

Originally published by the United States Conference of Catholic Bishops' Committee on Catechesis in the Fall of 2008 as a parish resource to be distributed on Catechetical Sunday.

Or it could mean both at the same time.

Our words about the Word can seem complicated or contradictory. Yet they're no small matter for us, since we are talking here about the love, the commands, the message, and the very person of the God who made us and saved us.

What does the Church mean when it speaks of the Word of God? What does God mean when He speaks of His Word?

All Together Now

I took up these questions in 2008 at the request of the United States Conference of Catholic Bishops, as the Church prepared for the October 2008 Synod on "The Word of God in the Life and Mission of the Church."

For two years beforehand, theologians had prepared for the Synod and in their preliminary document (called a *lineamenta*) they took up the problem of the multiple meanings of "The Word of God."

And not only did they take it up, they showed us why it's not really a problem at all. It was a master stroke, really. In their title for Section 9 of the document, they employed a beautiful phrase. They spoke of "The Word of God as a Symphony."

A symphony: When we think of God's Word in this way, we come to understand the diversity of meanings in a different and better way.

What is a symphony? It's a piece of music scored for many different instruments, all "sounding together"— that's the root of the Greek *symphonia*. In a symphony, various elements combine in unison and harmony. Winds, percussion, brass, and strings are not contradictory, but rather complementary. They blend together to make music that inspires us to great love, contemplation, and action.

This comparison of "the Word" to a symphony became popular a generation ago, around the time of the Second Vatican Council (1962–65). In the years following Vatican II, a German theologian named Joseph Ratzinger took up the metaphor, explaining that the symphony of faith is a "melody composed of the many, apparently discordant strains in the contrapuntal interplay of law, prophets, Gospel, and apostles."[1] That German theologian, of course, would one day become the man who summoned the 2008 Synod, Pope Benedict XVI.

Fully Divine, Fully Human

The Word of God resounds like a symphony. There is nothing monotonous about it. God has spoken to us "in many and various ways" (Heb. 1:1). He speaks to us in the wonders of creation; for He made all the universe through His eternal Word (Jn. 1:3). He speaks to us in the written story of creation and salvation that we find in the Bible—in the law, prophets, Gospel, and apostles.

Yet all these various strains harmonize perfectly in the person of the Word made flesh, Jesus Christ. The *Catechism of the Catholic Church* echoes St. Augustine as it explains: "Through all the words of Sacred Scripture, God speaks only one single Word, his one Utterance in whom he expresses himself completely [cf. Heb. 1:1–3]" (Catechism,

---

[1] Joseph Cardinal Ratzinger, *The Nature and Mission of Theology: Approaches to Understanding Its Role in the Light of Present Controversy*, trans. Adrian Walker (San Francisco: Ignatius, 1995), 84.

no. 102). Jesus Himself is the revealed Word of God, and He in turn has revealed Himself to be the subject of "all the Scriptures" (see Lk. 24:27). All of the Bible is about Him, even the parts that were written many centuries before He was born. It is Jesus who makes the Bible one book, and even "one Word."

For Jesus truly, completely, and perfectly embodies the Word of God. That's what we mean when we speak of the truth at the heart of our faith: the Incarnation. "The Word became flesh and made his dwelling among us" (Jn. 1:14).

In that event, God communicated Himself completely. Yet even then He spoke to us in words. Jesus spoke. He preached. He counseled. He taught. He prayed aloud. He asked questions. He told stories. He even traced words in the sand. He did all of this for our sake, because words are a normal human thing. Nevertheless, His words are extraordinary, because they are revelatory. They are human words that reveal the eternal Word of God. They are the Word of God in the words of men and women and children.

Beginning with this premise, the document for the Synod encourages us to think of "the Word" in this "analogous sense." We may look for relations of resemblance between the Word inspired (Scripture) and the Word incarnate (Jesus).

Both are fully divine and fully human. Jesus is true God and true man. He is coeternal with the Father; yet He was born of the Virgin Mary. St. Thomas Aquinas said that "Christ's humanity is the instrument of his divinity." In a similar way, the words of the Bible are instruments of the Word of God. Tradition speaks of the Scriptures as

4

"the Word of God in the words of men." Yet, in both the Incarnation and the inspiration, the divine agent and the human instrument are inseparably united.

In Jesus, God's Word became "a man like us in all things but sin" (Eucharistic Prayer IV). In Scripture, God's Word is expressed in human words, but without the fallible qualities we usually associate with human literature. It is inspired by God, authored by God, and so it is given a certain authority by God. In the words of the *lineamenta*, "Through the charism of divine inspiration, the Books of Sacred Scripture have a direct, concrete power of appeal not possessed by other texts of holy writings."

Both the Incarnation and the inspiration of the Word are divinely revealed mysteries, known only by faith. We could never demonstrate them simply by logic or science. We could not have known them apart from God's revelation and the gift of faith.

The Word in Full

So important are our Scriptures that they are sometimes misrepresented as the centerpiece of our religion. Journalists and even scholars will sometimes characterize Christianity as a "religion of the book."

But that's a misunderstanding. In fact, the *Catechism* explicitly rejects that idea, stating clearly that "the Christian faith is *not* a 'religion of the book.'" Then it goes on to make the necessary distinction: "Christianity is the religion of the 'Word' of God, 'not a written and mute word, but incarnate and living' [St. Bernard, *S. missus est hom.* 4, 11: PL 183, 86]" (Catechism, no. 108).

We encounter not a dead letter, but a person: the "Word of God ... living and active" (Heb. 4:12). This is not a word we can manipulate or spin to suit our whims. It is Jesus Christ, who comes with a fearsome power over all the elements, over life and death. "His eyes are like a flame of fire, and on his head are many diadems. . . . He is clad in a robe dipped in blood, and the name by which he is called is The Word of God" (Rev. 19:12–13).

The Church, in preparation for the synod in 2008, wanted to ensure that we made no mistake about it. Our religion is not reducible to the printed pages of our sacred book. The *lineamenta* warns us to avoid "erroneous or over-simplistic approaches and any ambiguity."

Instead, we are invited to listen to the Word of God in all its symphonic richness. The Word comes to us in the Scriptures, yes, but also in the life and Sacred Tradition of our community of faith. This is how the first Christians received the Word of God. Their faith was certainly not reducible to a book, because there was not yet a book for them to read. They had no New Testament; it had yet to be written. It would take centuries, in fact, before the New Testament was published as a single book. What's more, very few of those early Christians could read well enough to study even the Old Testament, and still fewer could afford to own books in those long-ago years before the printing press.

But they all—regardless of income or abilities—received the living Word of God in the heart of the Church. They received the Word in His Body, alive on earth, the Church. St. Paul makes clear that the written text was just one way the Word lived in the Church. He told the Thessalonians:

"Stand firm and hold to the traditions which you were taught by us, either by word of mouth or by letter" (2 Thess. 2:15). So, for Paul and his hearers, Tradition and "word of mouth" were as authoritative as Holy Writ. The life of the Church was much more than a book study. It was the life Christ gave to the apostles, the living faith of the Catholic Church.

Again, we see in the New Testament that the apostles gave the Christian Church so much more than texts. They passed on rituals (see 1 Cor. 11:23); they pronounced blessings (Acts 6:6); they conveyed authority (Acts 13:3); they healed the sick (Acts 28:8). The Second Vatican Council speaks of the fullness of Christian living—the fullness of the Tradition—the fullness of the *symphony*: "Now what was handed on by the Apostles includes everything which contributes toward the holiness of life and increase in faith of the peoples of God; and so the Church, in her teaching, life and worship, perpetuates and hands on to all generations all that she herself is, all that she believes" (*Dei Verbum*, no. 8).

Mass Media

But it's fair for us to askzzz How did it all happen? Where did it all happen for those first Christians?

We ask because we know that the answer to those questions should have some bearing on the way we receive the Word of God today.

The New Testament makes clear that there was indeed a place where the Church ordinarily encountered the Word. There was a place where the Scriptures were regularly proclaimed, and the rites enacted in the customary ways.

There was a place where the apostles normally preached and where the congregation read the apostolic letters aloud.

That place was the liturgy. Twice in the second chapter of the Acts of the Apostles, we read about "the breaking of the bread" as the distinctive Christian activity. "And they devoted themselves to the apostles' teaching and fellowship, to the breaking of bread and the prayers" (Acts 2:42). The motif recurs often afterward, and it continues throughout the surviving documents of those early centuries. The early Church was a Eucharistic Church.

In the ritual public worship of the Church, Christians encountered the Word of God. It was not simplistic; it was symphonic. The people received the Word of God present in the inspired Scriptures, proclaimed in the readings from the Old Testament and the New. They received the Word of God in the inspired preaching of Christ's priests. The people received the Word of God in His true flesh as they received the sacramental elements. They received the Word of God in His Body, the assembled Church.

Indeed, it is by the Word of God that bread can be transformed into the very flesh of Christ and that mere mortals can be transformed into Christ's immortal Body.

How can that be? How can a Word possess such power? Let's return to our analogy. God's Word is like our words in many ways. It is expressive and informative. But God's Word is unlike ours, too, because it is divine. Our words merely stand for things. When I speak of roses, I may evoke a bouquet in your imagination, but my words lack the power to drop even a single petal into your hand.

God's Word, on the other hand, has the power to accomplish the very things that it signifies. You and I write words on paper. But God writes the world the way we write words. He does so simply by the power of His Word: "[H]e commanded and they were created" (Ps. 148:5).

The Word in its fullness is a powerful thing. It is, as I said before, a fearsome thing. But that, too, is a quality of great symphonies. Beethoven's fifth and ninth will shake us to our souls if we let them. A great composer can stoke the fires of love and courage. A great composer can rouse a nation with a song. A great composer can drive us to mighty deeds.

But all that is nothing compared to what God wants to accomplish through His Word. God wants us to be, in Christ, a new creation. We do not merely *hear* the eternal Word. We are baptized into the very life of the eternal Word. We come to "become partakers of the divine nature" (2 Pet. 1:4). We participate in the symphony, not as spectators or listeners, but as performers. We speak it. We pray the Word. We ponder it. We make the Word our own through our full, conscious, and active participation in the liturgy. And then we take that Word out into the world. The Word makes us His own. He gives us His flesh and blood to be our own.

So that great and fearsome life is not just something "out there" in heaven. It is the very life we live today as children of God. For the Word of God is the Son of God by nature, and it is that very nature He came to share with us through the Church. It's His life that we receive from the Church, and it's His life that we live in the Church, in all its symphonic richness.

Let it shake you like no symphony ever has. Let the tympani rattle your soul and bring you to your feet in glory and praise. Like Paul, I want to tell you a mystery (1 Cor. 15:51) and, indeed, many mysteries all at once. For there is mystery enough for everyone to possess and to enjoy. As St. Thomas Aquinas said, the Scriptures contain "many senses under one letter," the better to suit the full range of intellectual gifts in the human race—"so that everyone," he explained, "may marvel that he is able to find in Sacred Scripture the truth that he has mentally conceived."

It's a mystery that human words can be inspired as they are in the Sacred Scriptures. It's a mystery that the Divine Word could become incarnate and dwell among us. It's a mystery that we can share in a Word that is infinite and eternal, though we are finite and mortal.

But that's the mystery God has given us. It's the Word from above, but it's also the Word on the street. And that, in a Word, is the good news.

The Person and Prayer of Jesus:
Reflections on the Biblical Christology of Pope Benedict XVI

Comparisons are odious, and contrasts are hardly better. But they arise in the mind unbidden in the early years of a pontificate. One pope's ministry is the immediate context for the next pope's ministry. We cannot help but examine one pontiff's doctrine and vision, his choices and omissions, in the light of the doctrine and vision, choices and omissions of his immediate predecessor.

A biblical theologian is doubly predisposed to seek out typological patterns in the divine economy.

And so I ask you to indulge me as I draw a comparison between the legacy of Pope John Paul II and the future legacy of Pope Benedict XVI.

In the early years of his pontificate, from September 1979 to November 1984, Pope John Paul II delivered a series of lectures at his Wednesday audiences. They were difficult, deeply philosophical, and drew from many different disciplines. They ranged from the moral to the metaphysical as they treated matters of human sexuality. Those 129 lectures have since come to be known as the "Theology of the Body."

Given as the semi-annual Pope Benedict XVI Lecture at St. Vincent Seminary, Latrobe, Pennsylvania, December 4, 2007.

But at the time, they were hardly known at all. Even though the subject matter was of perennial and universal interest—we're talking about sex, after all—the media only took notice once, when Pope John Paul made the hardly disputable observation that a married man could be guilty of lustful thoughts about his own wife.

It was surely a slow news day.

A lot has changed since then. The Theology of the Body gradually entered the mainstream, and has even become a popular movement in the Church. It's the subject of best-selling books and tape series, parish discussion groups, and even freshman-orientation programs at Catholic schools.

In 1999, Pope John Paul's biographer George Weigel described the Theology of the Body as "one of the boldest reconfigurations of Catholic theology in centuries"—"a kind of theological time bomb set to go off with dramatic consequences … perhaps in the 21st century."[1] Weigel predicted that it would reshape the Church's "theology, preaching, and religious education," compelling "a dramatic development of thinking about virtually every major theme in the Creed."[2]

I believe that's true, and I believed it when I first read those lectures, as a Protestant minister in the early 1980s.

But I have not come here today to talk about the Theology of the Body. I bring it up as a point of comparison, because I believe Pope Benedict is also setting a "theological time bomb set to go off with dramatic consequences"—an explosive doctrine that could reshape theology, preaching, and religious education. But it's not

---

[1] George Weigel, *Witness to Hope* (San Francisco: Harper, 1999), 343.
[2] Weigel, *Witness to Hope*, 853.

about sex this time. It's about Christ. It may be many years before we see the dramatic consequences, but I think we can already reckon the power and force of Benedict's great project. It is, to use his term, a "biblical Christology."

It is not, however, something new with Benedict. It was, for many decades, the theological labor, slowly and meticulously developed, of one Joseph Ratzinger. It emerges inchoately in his varied work as preacher, scholar, bishop, and prefect of the Congregation for the Doctrine of the Faith. Perhaps it is coming to its mature form in his projected multivolume work *Jesus of Nazareth*.

As Professor Ratzinger, and as Cardinal Ratzinger, and as Pope Benedict, our subject has been a prolific author. His works fill shelves, and his biblical Christology represents no small portion of that body of work. So it would be impossible for us to attempt an overview tonight. Since we have time to consider only one aspect of Pope Benedict's biblical Christology, I would like to go directly to the heart of the matter—to the element that Benedict himself has identified as the heart of his biblical Christology: the person and prayer of Jesus.

• • • • •

Christology is a "word about Christ"—a wisdom about Christ—a doctrine or even knowledge of Christ. It is the formal, intellectual development of the most basic thought process of any man, woman, or child who is consciously Christian. We think about Jesus, His mission, message, and meaning.

The Church is heir to centuries of this reflection, carried on by saints and scholars—and sometimes even by academics who are saints. But progress in the field is not simply progressive and cumulative. Theology proceeds by fits and starts, and sometimes it recedes or breaks down.

Where are we now? Joseph Ratzinger has spoken of the current state of Christology in terms of "crisis."[3] Just a few months before his elevation to the papacy, he wrote that "Christology has been losing its meaning."[4]

Elsewhere, he observed that theological debate no longer took place within a common framework or with a common language. Before the council, theologians could begin from a shared foundation of dogmatic assumptions and scholastic terms. But "now," Cardinal Ratzinger said, the "fundamentals themselves are widely matters of dispute."[5]

He traces the causes of the crisis to certain trends in critical exegesis—to biblical interpreters who "thought that everything supernatural, everything pertaining to the mystery of God that surrounded Jesus, was merely the embellishment and exaggeration of believers."[6]

According to this view, "Only with everything supernatural removed could the true figure of Jesus finally come to view!"

Cardinal Ratzinger recognized a noble impulse at the origin of these trends. "It started," he said, "with the effort to rediscover the man Jesus behind the gilded background

---

[3] See, for example, his introduction to Romano Guardini's *The Lord* (Washington: Regnery, 1996), xi.
[4] Joseph Cardinal Ratzinger, *On the Way to Jesus Christ*, trans. Michael J. Miller (San Francisco: Ignatius, 2005), 7.
[5] Joseph Cardinal Ratzinger, *Behold the Pierced One*, trans. Graham Harrison (San Francisco: Ignatius, 1986), 13.
[6] Ratzinger, "Introduction," Guardini, *The Lord*, xi.

of dogma, to return to the simplicity of the Gospels."[7] Both theologians and exegetes ceased speaking of "Christ" as they turned increasingly to "Jesus." This, of course, required a violent separation of the biblical text from the Church's tradition of reflection and interpretation. And this is what precipitated the crisis.

To maneuver around "Christ" to get to "Jesus" might seem like a shortcut to greater intimacy. But what we find is that, apart from a hermeneutic of faith—apart from the Church's confession of the Christ—Jesus becomes indistinct. He is, as the cardinal noted, "continually splitting into new pictures of Jesus. There is the Jesus of the logia, the Jesus of this or that community, Jesus the philanthropist, Jesus the Jewish rabbi, the apocalyptic Jesus, Jesus the Zealot, Jesus the revolutionary, the political Jesus, et cetera."[8]

The man who witnessed such a breakdown in Christology might be excused if he had simply taken to the trenches with a reactionary and exaggerated scholasticism. But that was not Benedict's response. Indeed, he seemed to welcome the return to Jesus by way of the biblical sources. With quiet confidence, he noted that "Catholic dogma ... derives all its content from Scripture."[9] He took up the challenge of a return to theology's primary referential language, and he engaged the questions that faced Christology in a new generation.

---

[7] Ratzinger, *On the Way to Jesus Christ*, 7.
[8] Ratzinger, *Behold the Pierced One*, 44.
[9] Joseph Cardinal Ratzinger, "Cardinal Frings's Speeches during the Second Vatican Council: Some Reflections Apropos of Muggeridge's The Desolate City," *Communio*, Spring 1988, 136.

• • • • •

What were those questions? They were essentially different, he said, from the preoccupations of the preconciliar generation. Before the council, theologians gravitated toward the systematic treatment of the hypostatic union or Christ's knowledge. Afterward, more were asking, "'How is the christological dogma related to the testimony of Scripture?' and 'What is the relationship between biblical Christology, in its several phases of development, and the figure of the real historical Jesus?'"

In an important address delivered in 1982, he attempted to establish a solid framework for future development of a biblical Christology. In its published form, titled "Taking Bearings in Christology," he proposed seven theses as a common ground. The first of these seven is fundamental. It is this: "According to the testimony of Holy Scripture, the center of the life and person of Jesus is his constant communication with the Father."[10]

It is a simple observation that seems obvious, once stated. Of all the roles and relations Jesus has in the New Testament, one is primary and that is His sonship. Before all else—before priest, prophet, king, lord, and even christ—He is Son. Cardinal Ratzinger comments: "The title 'Son' comes in the end to be the only, comprehensive designation for Jesus. It both comprises and interprets everything else."[11]

---

[10] Ratzinger, *Behold the Pierced One*, 15.
[11] Ibid., 16.

Jesus' sonship is primary because it is eternal, whereas all His other roles and relations are temporal. Only after there is a creation can Christ be Lord of creation. Only for human hearers can He serve as prophet. Only over earthly subjects can He rule as king.

He is Son, however, from all eternity.

Thus, His core identity is always relational. He lives in relation to the Father, in communication with the Father. Cardinal Ratzinger said: "In all the words and deeds of Jesus, this filial relationship always shines through, ever-present and ever-creative; we perceive that his whole being is at home in this relationship."[12]

All of Jesus' actions flow from His relationship with the Father. Cardinal Ratzinger observes that "the essential events of Jesus' activity proceeded from the core of his personality and … this core was his dialogue with the Father."[13] The evangelists portray this vividly as they show Jesus going "into the hills" to pray (see Mk. 1:35; 6:46; 14:35, 39). His "words and deeds flowed from his most intimate communion with the Father."[14]

One thing we can say with certainty of the historical Jesus: His life was prayer. This is true whether we consider Him as rabbi, sage, or revolutionary. His primary role and relation is that of a Son in the presence of His Father.

Even the most extreme critics accept Jesus' sense of sonship as a historical fact, if only because it is so incongruous with the piety of His contemporaries. Those of us of a certain age will recall the much-publicized meeting of

---

[12] Ibid., 21.
[13] Ibid., 17.
[14] Ibid.

The Jesus Seminar, which concluded that the Aramaic word *Abba* was the only New Testament passage that could be indisputably traced to Jesus.

Well, at least on the matter of *that* word, we find Cardinal Ratzinger and The Jesus Seminar in perfect agreement. "The 'Abba' with which Jesus addresses God, which Mark has preserved for us in Jesus' Aramaic mother tongue, goes beyond every mode of prayer then known. It expresses a familiarity with God which would have appeared impossible and unseemly to the Jewish tradition. Thus this one, unique word expresses the new and unique manner of Jesus' relationship to God—a relationship which, on his own side, calls for the term 'Son' as the only possible one."[15]

Prayer is "the central act of the Person of Jesus and, indeed, . . . this person is constituted by the act of prayer, of unbroken communication with the one he calls 'Father.'"[16]

Jesus is the Son, and He spends His whole life in communion with the Father, in conversation with the Father. Prayer is the "core of his personality."[17] His identity is inseparable from His prayer. His very life is prayer, and, as Cardinal Ratzinger points out, "Jesus died praying. He fashioned his death into an act of prayer."[18]

In a lapidary phrase, the cardinal summed it up: "We see *who Jesus is* if we see him at prayer."[19]

---

[15] Ibid., 20–21.
[16] Ibid., 26.
[17] Ibid., 17–18.
[18] Ibid., 22.
[19] Ibid., 19.

• • • • •

Through this consideration of sonship, Cardinal Ratzinger demonstrated that the Church's dogma is never far from the page of Scripture. I mentioned earlier his assertion that "Catholic dogma ... derives all its content from Scripture."[20] Elsewhere, he states that "dogma is by definition nothing other than an interpretation of Scripture."[21] Dogma is the Church's infallible interpretation of the sacred text.

Thus there is no contradiction, no opposition, between the Jesus of history to the Christ of dogma. Indeed, the Jesus of history is unknowable except as the Christ of dogma, the anointed Son of the Father.

> In concentrating on "Son" as the comprehensive interpretative category for the figure of Jesus, the Church was responding precisely to the basic historical experience of those who had been eyewitnesses of Jesus' life. Calling Jesus the "Son," far from overlaying him with the mythical gold of dogma ... corresponds most strictly to the center of the historical figure of Jesus.[22]

The recovery of the word "Son" does not, by itself, represent a wholesale rehabilitation of the Church's dogmatic tradition. Yet it is a key element in the argument, and Cardinal Ratzinger applies it in an exemplary way to the

---

[20] Joseph Cardinal Ratzinger, "Cardinal Frings's Speeches during the Second Vatican Council," *Communio*, Spring 1988, 136.
[21] Joseph Cardinal Ratzinger, "Crisis in Catechetics," *Canadian Catholic Review*, June 1983, 178.
[22] Ratzinger, *Behold the Pierced One*, 17.

classic case of a dogmatic pronouncement—the Council of Nicaea's use of extra biblical, philosophical language in its definitions regarding the Incarnation.

The Council of Nicaea in 325 was the first ecumenical council, called to settle the Arian controversy. Arius contended that the Son was neither coeternal nor coequal with the Father, but rather an exalted creature, an adopted son. The council fathers ruled against Arius, stating that the Son is *homoousios* with the Father—that is, He is of the same substance with the Father or, as we say in the current liturgical translation, "one in being with the Father." The Arian party objected that the term *homoousios* was nowhere to be found in the Bible and thus was an inappropriate application of pagan terms to Christian theology.

But the Nicene dogma prevailed, of course. And, according to Cardinal Ratzinger, it prevailed precisely because the "dogma's basic assertion, 'the Son is of the same substance' … simply puts *the fact of Jesus' prayer* into the technical language of philosophical theology, nothing more."[23]

The fact … and nothing more.

Nothing more indeed! How could a word *hold* more meaning than that?

Take a moment to ponder what the future pope is saying. When we profess in the Creed that Jesus is "one in being with the Father," we are proclaiming that the Father and the Son live in an unbroken, eternal communion. *Homoousios* means "nothing more" than the perfect prayer of Jesus. *Homoousios* means "nothing more" than divine. *Homoousios* means "nothing more" than the Trinitarian and Incarnational doctrine that is implicit in the biblical text.

---

[23] Ibid., 33, emphasis added.

In case we missed his point the first time, the author restates it a few pages later: "What does 'of one substance' really mean? ... the term is used solely as a translation of the word 'Son' into philosophical language."[24]

And, with Nicaea, Cardinal Ratzinger emphasizes that Jesus' sonship is not metaphorical, but rather metaphysical. It is to be understood "in the most real and concrete sense of the word. The central word of the New Testament, the word 'Son,' is to be understood literally ... Jesus is not only described as the Son of God, he is the Son of God."[25]

And He is always at prayer. We profess and proclaim that His prayer constitutes His most basic personal identity: His relation to the Father.

Again, the case of Nicaea is classic, and it is exemplary. It prefigures and "summarizes the entire witness of the ancient councils."[26]

• • • • •

The great champion of the Nicene faith was St. Athanasius of Alexandria. Sometimes it seemed that he was the *only* champion. "Athanasius against the world"—that was the way his contemporaries sized up the situation. But why was Athanasius willing to take on the entire world? Why was he willing to suffer exile and imprisonment? Why was he willing to risk his life, just for that term *homoousios*? The moderates of his time proposed a compromise

---

[24] Ibid., 36.
[25] Ibid.
[26] Ibid.

term, with just one letter's difference, one *iota*'s difference. They proposed that both the orthodox and the Arians could truthfully profess that the Son was *homoiousios*, of *like* substance with the Father. Yet Athanasius rejected any compromise. Why?

Because the stakes were very high. If the Son were not true God from true God, then the very nature of our salvation was changed. God did not truly come to share our lot and share our suffering. Nor did He truly share His life with us in baptism. And that thought was unbearable to Athanasius—and to all the orthodox Fathers.

Cardinal Ratzinger draws our attention to a basic axiom of epistemology: "knowledge depends on a certain similarity between the knower and the known." It is only because God became man that we can dare to claim that similarity. Athanasius is one of many patristic witnesses, beginning with Irenaeus in the second century, to the "formula of exchange." Here is how Athanasius put the matter: "For he was made man that we might be made God," and "he himself has made us sons of the Father, and deified men by becoming himself man."[27]

We are deified—divinized. We are, in another classic formulation, "sons in the Son." What else could Jesus have meant when He quoted the Psalm and said, "You are gods"? What else could the Second Letter of Peter mean by the outrageous claim that we are "partakers of the divine nature" (2 Pet. 1:4)?

"Knowledge depends on a certain similarity between the knower and the known,"[28] and we have been given that

---

[27] Athanasius, *On the Incarnation*, no. 54.
[28] Ratzinger, *Behold the Pierced One*, 25.

similarity as an unmerited grace—the grace of filial deification, the grace of divine sonship. For the early Fathers, that was the *nature of salvation*. That was the *content of the Gospel*. And in the fourth century a single iota threatened to relegate God again to obscurity.

Like a modern Athanasius, Cardinal Ratzinger places filial deification at the center of his discussion. He does so, however, in his own distinctive way. He does so by speaking in terms of the prayer of Jesus.

He says, "Since the center of the person of Jesus is prayer, it is essential to participate in his prayer if we are to know and understand him."[29] When he says "participate," he's not merely asking us to sing along with gusto at worship. He's using the term in the sense of the Greek *koinonia*—the sense in which it is used in Second Peter and other New Testament texts. He's talking about a real participation, a sharing of divine life, a communion.

The consequences of this communion are breathtaking. In the book *Jesus of Nazareth*, Pope Benedict tells us that, by sharing His divine life, "Jesus … involves us in his own prayer; he leads us into the interior dialogue of triune love."[30] In his encyclical, *Spe Salvi*, he writes: "It is only by becoming children of God, that we can be with our common Father."[31] Thus, when we pray, we live the life of the Trinity, the life of heaven, even now!

It is in this context that the Holy Father examines the words of the Our Father, the perfect prayer. He says, "We

---

[29] Ibid.

[30] Pope Benedict XVI, *Jesus of Nazareth*, trans. Adrian J. Walker (New York: Doubleday, 2007), 132.

[31] Pope Benedict XVI, Encyclical, Saved In Hope *Spe Salvi* (November 30, 2007), 33.

must strive to recognize the thoughts Jesus wished to pass on to us in these words. But we must also keep in mind that the Our Father originates from his own praying, from the Son's dialogue with the Father. This means that it reaches down into depths far beyond the words … and can therefore never be fully fathomed by a purely historical exegesis."[32]

Jesus shares His prayer, which is His very life, with redeemed humanity. We are caught up into the very life of the Trinity. And we are divinized by the words of the prayer themselves. They conform our prayer to His and our life to His. His prayer becomes the form of our life, as it is the principle and substance of His own life. The Pope explains that Jesus' words in the Lord's Prayer "aim to configure us to the image of the Son. The meaning of the Our Father goes much further than the mere provision of a prayer text. It aims to form our being, to train us in the inner attitude of Jesus (cf. Phil. 2:5)."[33] "The Our Father does not project a human image onto heaven, but shows us from heaven—from Jesus—what we human beings can and should be like."[34]

That's *communion*. And that communion has profound implications for ecclesiology as well, because, in the words of Joseph Ratzinger, "Sharing in Jesus' praying involves communion with all his brethren."[35] In *Jesus of Nazareth*, Pope Benedict further elucidated this point: "When we say the word our [in the Our Father], we say 'yes' to the living Church in which the Lord wanted to gather his new family.

---

[32] Pope Benedict XVI, *Jesus of Nazareth*, 133.
[33] Ibid., 132.
[34] Ibid., 137.
[35] Ratzinger, *Behold the Pierced One*, 27.

In this sense, the Our Father is at once a fully personal and a thoroughly ecclesial prayer. In praying the Our Father, we pray totally with our own heart, but at the same time we pray in communion with the whole Family of God, with the living and the dead, with men and women of all conditions, cultures, and races. The Our Father overcomes all boundaries and makes us one family."[36]

To be fully alive in Jesus' prayer, then, we must be truly living in the Church. "[O]nly by entering into Jesus' solitude," Cardinal Ratzinger insists, "only by participating in what is most personal to him, his communication with the Father, can one see what this most personal reality is; only thus can one penetrate to his identity. . . . The person who has beheld Jesus' intimacy with his Father and has come to understand him from within is called to be a 'rock' of the Church. The Church arises out of participation in the prayer of Jesus."[37]

I feel compelled at this point to turn to our most ordinary participation in the prayer of Jesus—in the Church's liturgy.

Dignum et iustum est. For Pope Benedict himself calls forth the witness of St. Benedict as he sets forth his doctrine on our sharing in the prayer of Christ. Allow me to quote at length from *Jesus of Nazareth*:

In his Rule, St. Benedict coined the formula *Mens nostra concordet voci nostrae*—our mind must be in accord with our voice (Rule, 19, 7). Normally, thought precedes word; it seeks and formulates the word. But praying the Psalms and liturgical prayer in general is exactly the

---

[36] Pope Benedict XVI, *Jesus of Nazareth*, 141.
[37] Ratzinger, *Behold the Pierced One*, 19.

other way round: The word, the voice, goes ahead of us, and our mind must adapt to it. For on our own we human beings do not "know how to pray as we ought" (Rom. 8:26)—we are too far removed from God, he is too mysterious and too great for us. And so God has come to our aid: He himself provides the words of our prayer and teaches us to pray. Through the prayers that come from him, he enables us to set out toward him; by praying together with the brothers and sisters he has given us, we gradually come to know him and draw closer to him.

In St. Benedict's writings, the phrase cited just now refers directly to the Psalms, the great prayer book of the People of God of the Old and New Covenant. The Psalms are words that the Holy Spirit has given to men; they are God's Spirit become word. We thus pray "in the Spirit," with the Holy Spirit. This applies even more, of course, to the Our Father.[38]

We must keep in mind that Jesus' own prayer was not simply a wordless union with the Father. He prayed human words, the words of biblical faith. We know from the Gospels that He Himself prayed the Psalms, even with His dying breath. He prayed the She'ma: "Hear, O Israel …" He served as a lector in the synagogue liturgy.

We should imitate Him by the way we pray the Psalms and other formal prayers, vocal prayers. In *Spe Salvi*, Pope Benedict writes of Cardinal Van Thuan, the great modern confessor from Vietnam. A giant of the spiritual life, Cardinal Van Thuan said that, "when he was unable

---

[38] Pope Benedict XVI, *Jesus of Nazareth*, 131.

to pray ... he would hold fast to the texts of the Church's prayer: the Our Father, the Hail Mary and the prayers of the liturgy."[39]

Again in *Spe Salvi*, Pope Benedict notes that in "liturgical prayer ... the Lord teaches us again and again how to pray properly."[40]

Christ's prayers were often the simple prayers of His nation. In our simple formal prayers—the Our Father, the Hail Mary, the Glory Be, the Creed—we are one with Him, one with the prayer at the core of His being.

How much more, then, do we commune with Him—and with His prayer—when we celebrate the Mass, the Eucharistic liturgy, the source and summit of our participation in Jesus' life, Jesus' prayer?

Liturgy, Cardinal Ratzinger wrote, is "the place of encounter with Jesus. It is above all in the liturgy that Jesus is among us, here it is that he speaks to us, here he lives." He goes on to say: "liturgy is the true, living environment for the Bible, ... [and] the Bible can be properly understood only in this living context within which it first emerged. The texts of the Bible, this great book of Christ, are not to be seen as the literary products of some scribes at their desks, but rather as the words of Christ himself delivered in the celebration of holy Mass."[41]

Elsewhere, he put it this way: "[Since] prayer is central to the person of Jesus, sharing his prayer is the prerequisite for knowing and understanding him."[42]

---

[39] Pope Benedict XVI, *Spe Salvi*, no. 34.
[40] Ibid.
[41] Ratzinger, "Introduction," Guardini, *The Lord*, xii.
[42] Joseph Cardinal Ratzinger, *Journey Towards Easter: Retreat Given in the Vatican in the Presence of Pope John Paul II*, trans. Dame Mary Groves (New York: Crossroad, 1987), 122.

Nowhere is that sharing so profound and so powerful as in the Eucharist. That is what biblical Christology teaches us. That is what we learn from the texts of the Gospels themselves.

Cardinal Ratzinger did not tire of repeating that Jesus' life was prayer, and that "He fashioned his death into an act of prayer, an act of worship."[43] He institutionalized the giving of His Body, the pouring out of His Blood. He sacramentalized the prayer at the core of His person.

The Gospel makes clear that Jesus willed us to be in the Church. Moreover, He willed us to be at church on Sunday. A century ago, Alfred Loisy lamented that Jesus promised us a kingdom, but all He left us was the Church. Yet commentators from St. Augustine to Pope Benedict point out that this is a false opposition. The latter puts it succinctly: "the question of whether Jesus intended to found a Church is a false question because it is unhistorical. The only proper way to phrase the question would be to ask whether Jesus intended to abolish the People of God or to renew it. The answer to this question, rightly put, is plain: Jesus made the old People of God into a new People by adopting those who believe in him into the community of his own self (of his 'Body'). He achieved this by transforming his death into an act of prayer, an act of love, and thus by making himself communicable. . . . The words of Jesus have never been able to live and mediate life except in this communion"[44]—the communion of the Church.

---

[43] Ratzinger, *Behold the Pierced One*, 22.
[44] Ibid., 30.

This communion is a real presence, a communicable presence. Pope Benedict says: "We have seen that Jesus is the Kingdom of God in person. The Kingdom of God is present wherever he is present."[45] He is present with us when we are at prayer, and He too is at prayer, and then we see most clearly who He is.

"We see who Jesus is if we see him at prayer."[46] We see who Jesus is when He makes Himself communicable to us. He makes His nature one with ours. He gives us everything He has—His Body, Blood, Soul, and Divinity—so that we might take them as our own. He makes His prayer one with ours, taking up what is ours and elevating it as His own.

"We see who Jesus is if we see him at prayer." And we must imitate Him, if we are truly to understand and share the biblical Christology of Pope Benedict XVI. For, as Benedict himself put it: "Real advances in Christology … can never come merely as the result of the theology of the schools. . . . It must be complemented by the theology of the saints, which is theology from experience. All real progress in theological understanding has its origin in the eye of love and in its faculty of beholding."[47]

These truths are at the heart of Pope Benedict's biblical Christology. They are indeed explosive. Give them time.

---

[45] Pope Benedict XVI, *Jesus of Nazareth*, 146.
[46] Ratzinger, *Behold the Pierced One*, 19.
[47] Ibid., 27.

Chapter Three

The Hermeneutic of Faith:
Pope Benedict XVI on Scripture, Liturgy, and Church

I like to seize upon those occasions when I can make common cause with the *New York Times*. On Easter Sunday 2007, the paper published a profile of Pope Benedict XVI. As a piece of journalism, it was spotty, but one line at least was immaculate in its truth-telling: "Benedict is one of the most intellectual men ever to serve as pope—and surely one of the most intellectual of current world leaders."[1]

It's a rather plain statement, but it speaks a truth that's easy for us Catholics to miss. We have been conditioned to evaluate churchmen as if they're influential politicians—either liberal or conservative. We're at ease thinking of the pontiff as a kind of ceremonial prop—the body that fills the necessary vestments. We're even happy to tout our Holy Father as the conscience of the world—the lone voice that will dare to scold the warlike and speak the truth to power.

But even after the papacy of Karol Wojtyla, the influential phenomenologist, we're unaccustomed to consider our pope as the *intellectual* leader of the world. Yet, thanks to

---

Given as the semi-annual Pope Benedict XVI Lecture at St. Vincent Seminary, Latrobe, Pennsylvania, April 18, 2007.
[1] Russell Shorto, "Keeping the Faith," *New York Times Magazine*, April 8, 2007.

the *New York Times*, we are confronted with the fact. And it is no mere assertion. It is recognition of a body of work that many of Benedict's fellow theologians have recognized for decades.

It has been noted that never before in the history of the Church has a world-renowned theologian and biblical scholar of Benedict's stature been elevated to the papacy. The election of Pope Benedict XVI, in 2005, brought to the Chair of St. Peter one of the world's finest theological minds, a public intellectual long engaged in dialogue over the crucial issues of the modern period. And he genuinely engages his partners in conversation. Indeed, his appreciation for the Hebrew Scriptures and rabbinic interpretation has opened him to deep friendship with some of the great rabbis of our own age.

Joseph Ratzinger was a young academic theologian with a bright future when, in 1977, he was chosen to be archbishop of Munich and Freising. At the time, he identified a continuity between his scholarly work and his new service in the hierarchy of the Church. He took for his episcopal motto a biblical expression: "cooperators in the truth."[2]

In practical terms, however, his beginnings as a bishop brought an end to his promising career as an academic. He

---

[2] In explaining his episcopal motto, which is found in 3 John 8, he has said that "it seemed to be the connection between my previous task as teacher and my new mission. Despite all the differences in modality, what is involved was and remains the same: to follow the truth, to be at its service. And, because in today's world the theme of truth has all but disappeared, because truth appears to be too great for man and yet everything falls apart if there is no truth; for these reasons, this motto also seemed timely in the good sense of the word." Joseph Cardinal Ratzinger, *Milestones: Memoirs, 1927–1977*, trans. Erasmo Leiva-Merkiakis (San Francisco: Ignatius, 1998), 153.

would seldom again have the opportunity for sustained scholarly research and writing.[3] Nonetheless, in the last quarter-century, Benedict has produced a substantial body of work—articles, speeches, homilies, and more—that reflect the wide range of his study and interests, and the keen, systematic nature of his thought.

Had Professor Ratzinger been left to pursue his scholarly interests, his achievements would surely have rivaled or surpassed those of the greatest theologians of the last century—figures such as Hans Urs von Balthasar and Karl Rahner. For there has been no other Catholic theologian in the last century whose theology is as highly developed and systematically integrated in explicitly biblical terms. Indeed, we would be hard pressed to identify another thinker who has allowed Sacred Scripture to shape and direct his theologizing more than Cardinal Ratzinger.

Benedict's command of the biblical texts, the interpretive tradition of the Church Fathers, and the findings of historical and literary scholarship, represents the full flowering of the Catholic biblical renewal promoted by the popes and culminating in *Dei Verbum*, the Second Vatican Council's constitution on divine revelation. The first half of the twentieth century was marked by the *emergence* of three renewal movements—the biblical, the patristic, and the liturgical. We saw the *convergence* of those movements

---

[3] In forewords or afterwords to collections of his articles and talks, he sometimes expresses disappointment that his professional obligations make it impossible to develop his ideas as systematically or with the depth and precision that he would like. See, for example, Joseph Cardinal Ratzinger, *The Nature and Mission of Theology: Essays to Orient Theology in Today's Debates*, trans. Adrian Walker (San Francisco: Ignatius, 1995), 8.

in *Dei Verbum*. And now, in the theology of Benedict, we see their integration and coordination. Benedict has articulated a theology—a *biblical* theology—that synthesizes modern scientific methods with the ancient art of spiritual exegesis, an art that we encounter in the New Testament writers and Church Fathers, and which has continued throughout the Church's tradition.[4]

He has used the term "the authority of mystery"[5] in speaking of the Church's liturgy. But the phrase expresses just as well his integral vision of the Church as the handmaiden of the Word of God. The Church, as he sees it, lives under the authority of mystery—in dialogue with the Word that revealed the mystery of God's saving plan in history, and in obedient service to the Word as it seeks final accomplishment of God's plan in the life and age of the Church.

What is the foundation for Benedict's biblical theology? How does he reflect on the nature of Scripture and the function and mission of theology and exegesis in the Church? What is his method, so to speak? A fundamental premise is the interwoven unity of the Word of God and the People of God. He begins with the historical record

---

[4] For the purposes of this paper, I will be considering almost exclusively the theological opinions and insights that Benedict articulated prior to his pontificate. I will restrict myself to articles and addresses authored under his own name and will not consider decisions or other writings issued in his official capacity as prefect of the Vatican's Congregation for the Doctrine of the Faith. The theological and exegetical judgments and conclusions discussed herein, while reflective of and in accord with Catholic dogma and teaching, are not necessarily considered binding on Catholics.

[5] Joseph Cardinal Ratzinger, *A New Song for the Lord: Faith in Christ and Liturgy Today*, trans. Martha M. Matesich (New York: Crossroad Herder, 1997), 32.

of early Christianity and then describes a Church that is called into being by Christ's Gospel and by the salvation-historical event of His death and Resurrection.

He speaks of "the *memoria Ecclesiae* … the Church as memory."[6] It is the memory of Christ's saving actions that gives the Church its "common identity as God's family"[7]—and that memory is preserved in the written testimony of Scripture and renewed in the Church's sacramental liturgy. As the "living, historical subject" of God's Word,[8] the Church lives by and for the Word, bearing witness to the Word that others might experience its saving power.

This notion of the Church as living voice—this notion of the Church as memory—distinguishes Benedict's ideas about Tradition. He holds to the Church's ancient understanding. He believes that divine revelation is reserved not

---

[6] "Christian faith, by its very nature, includes the act of remembering; in this way, it brings about the unity of history and the unity of man before God, or rather: it can bring about the unity of history because God has given it memory. The seat of all faith is, then, the *memoria Ecclesiae*, the memory of the Church, the Church as memory. It exists through all ages, waxing and waning but never ceasing to be the common situs of faith." Joseph Cardinal Ratzinger, *Principles of Catholic Theology: Building Stones for a Fundamental Theology*, trans. Mary F. McCarthy (San Francisco: Ignatius, 1987), 23.

[7] Joseph Cardinal Ratzinger, *Gospel, Catechesis, Catechism: Sidelights on the Catechism of the Catholic Church* (San Francisco: Ignatius, 1997), 63.

[8] Joseph Cardinal Ratzinger, *The Spirit of the Liturgy*, trans. John Saward (San Francisco: Ignatius, 2000), 168. "The faith of the Church does not exist as an ensemble of texts, rather, the texts—the words—exist because there is a corresponding subject which gives them their basis and their inner coherence. Empirically speaking, the preaching of the apostles called into existence the social organization 'Church' as a kind of historical subject. One becomes a believer by joining this community of tradition, thought, and life, by living personally from its continuity of life throughout history, and by acquiring a share in its way of understanding, its speech and its thought." Joseph Cardinal Ratzinger, *The Nature and Mission of Theology: Essays to Orient Theology in Today's Debates*, trans. Adrian Walker (San Francisco: Ignatius, 1995), 94.

only to the written Word of God, but includes the Sacred Tradition handed on in the Church's teachings, sacramental worship, and life of faith.[9] Benedict, however, identifies a deeper dynamic—a dynamic of dialogue—as characteristic of the relationship between the Word and the Church.

Tradition, he argues, cannot be reduced to a treasure chest. It's not merely a static collection of ancient texts, and laws, and venerable practices. Rather, it's a living dialogue in which the Church constantly listens to the Word addressed to her. But it is indeed *a dialogue*, so the Church *responds* to the claims that the Word of God makes on her life. The Church's response to the Word—its preaching and proclamation, its teachings and liturgical life—forms the "stuff" of Tradition. But Tradition is still more than these things. Tradition is nothing other than the fulfillment of Christ's promise to be with His Church until the end of the age (Mt. 28:20). It is Christ's permanent, living, and saving presence in the Church.

The Holy Father sums it up this way, in slightly more technical language: "For the Catholic Christian, two lines of essential hermeneutic orientation assert themselves here. The first: we trust Scripture and we base ourselves on Scriptures, not on hypothetical reconstructions which go behind it. . . . The second is that we read Scripture in the living community of the Church, and therefore on the basis of the fundamental decisions thanks to which it has become historically efficacious, namely, those which laid the foundations of the Church. One must not separate the

---

[9] For a classical treatment of the relationship between Scripture and Tradition, see *Dei Verbum*, no. 7–10.

text from this living context. In this sense, Scripture and Tradition form an inseparable whole."[10]

Tradition, then, is a sort of ongoing divine intervention in history, an act of God that gives every succeeding generation the same contact with the risen Christ experienced by the first disciples. This experience, a true and personal encounter with the saving presence of Christ, forms the "content" of the Church's Tradition. And bringing about this encounter constitutes the mission of the Church.

In the Church's proclamation and liturgy, the Word of salvation spoken 2,000 years ago is always "a present reality."[11] It's not a museum piece or a curio. It's never a bygone we can let be bygone. In the words of Pope Benedict, the Church's sacraments give us nothing less than "*contemporaneity* with Christ."[12] In the sacraments, we are His contemporaries. Indeed, the Church's identity is defined in the Eucharist, which is a liturgical remembrance of the very saving event that the Word speaks of. And this remembrance was mandated by Christ Himself at the Last Supper. As Benedict points out: in this "solemn remembrance, *the means of salvation history*—the death and Resurrection of the Lord—is truly present."[13]

---

[10] Joseph Cardinal Ratzinger, "The Theology of the Liturgy," in *The Essential Pope Benedict XVI: His Central Writings and Speeches*, eds. John F. Thornton and Susan B. Varenne (San Francisco: Harper, 2007), 144–146.

[11] Joseph Cardinal Ratzinger, *Called to Communion: Understanding the Church Today*, trans. Adrian Walker (San Francisco: Ignatius, 1996 [1991]), 19.

[12] Ratzinger, *The Nature and Mission of Theology*, 60; Ratzinger, *Principles of Catholic Theology*, 88, 100.

[13] Ratzinger, *Principles of Catholic Theology*, 2. Emphasis added. See also, Joseph Cardinal Ratzinger, *Church, Ecumenism and Politics: New Essays in Ecclesiology*, trans. Robert Nowell and Fridesiwide Sandeman (New York: Crossroad, 1988), 8.

We see, then, that Benedict proceeds from a historical reconstruction of primitive Christianity. And in those first Christian generations, he discovers that the Church's missionary, liturgical, legal, and organizational aspects are integrally related. They all work together. We see, further, that his reconstruction recognizes the early Church's belief that it was guided, and even "in-dwelt," by the presence or Spirit of Christ. And we see that the Church's original mission and Tradition, again under the presence and tutelage of the Spirit, are ordered to liturgy—to the entrance of the believer into the Family of God through Word and sacrament.

Benedict's historical study also draws out the original work of the Word in the Church's missionary, catechetical, and confessional efforts. He notices that the faith itself is not simply an intellectual acceptance of a set of principles or ideas. The faith requires from each believer "a word about the Word"—a personal profession of faith in the Word that he or she has heard.[14]

Furthermore, Benedict notes that the confession of faith itself, the Creed, is an interpretive synthesis of the *biblical* testimony. It is a distillation of the Gospel, by which the Church determined "what actually constituted Christianity."[15] Profession of the Creed, from the start, was preceded by a period of preparation, a *catechumenate*, a time of instruction in the basic truths of the faith.[16] It was in the context of the Church's catechesis that many

---

[14] Ratzinger, *Gospel, Catechesis, Catechism*, 30–31.

[15] Ratzinger, *Principles of Catholic Theology*, 149.

[16] "Hand in hand with the sign there was always the instruction, the Word, that gave the sign its place in the history of Israel's covenant with God." Ratzinger, *Principles of Catholic Theology*, 29.

of its doctrinal formulas first arose.[17] But, again, that teaching, that catechesis, was fundamentally scriptural, built on a canonical belief in the unity of the Old and New Testaments.

In fact, Benedict helps us to see how the original confession of faith presumes not only a belief in the unity of Scripture—Old Testament and New—but also a belief that Scripture is to be interpreted in light of the cross and Resurrection of Christ. In its simplest form, the Christian confession is summarized in the name "Jesus Christ." In this confession, Jesus, the historical figure whose life and deeds are recorded in the New Testament, is acknowledged to be the "Christ," that is, the anointed messiah foretold in the Old Testament. Benedict concludes from this that confession of faith in Jesus Christ, the very bedrock of "Christian identity … is founded on the unity of the testaments."[18]

Again, he observes that the Church's most ancient practices cannot truly be understood without reference to its faith in the saving presence of Christ. The Sacrament of Baptism, like the Eucharist, is believed to be a true and real initiation into the salvation-historical event that is contained in the Word. The Church's sacraments, Benedict

---

[17] Ratzinger, *Principles of Catholic Theology*, 27. "To become a Christian is to enter into this one particular Creed, into the communal form of the faith. The inner bond between the community itself and this Creed is expressed by the fact that the acceptance into the community has the form of a sacrament: baptism and catechesis are inseparable. . . . By its very nature, the word of faith presupposes the community that lives it, that is bound to it, and adheres to it in its very power to bind mankind." Ratzinger, *Principles of Catholic Theology*, 329–330.

[18] Joseph Cardinal Ratzinger, *Many Religions, One Covenant: Israel, the Church and the World*, trans. Graham Harrison (San Francisco: Ignatius, 1999 [1998]), 18.

reminds us, are held to be "the communications of him who
… is God's visible Word."[19] By these acts, God establishes
with men and women a covenant, a family bond, making
them children in "the great family" of the Church.[20] In the
sacraments, the believer is united with God's larger salvific
design—"a common history in which God brought the
people together and became their way."[21]

With this historical foundation laid, we are ready to
consider Benedict's understanding of the task of theology
and biblical interpretation. For Benedict, the Church is
the living subject of theology. The Church is the "do-er"
of theology, because theology flows out of the Church's
remembrance. Theology flows from the Church's pondering, proclaiming, and "actualizing" of the Word of God.
Theology stems from the very structure of the faith, as a
consequence, even an imperative, of the faith. It begins in
the response to God's gift, the divine Word that God has
spoken to us in Jesus.[22] Theology is the believer's response
to the Word, who is a divine Person, and theology is, essentially, a reflection on the "contents" of the Word—the revelation of God's love, expressed in the new covenant made
in the death and Resurrection of Jesus Christ.

---

[19] Ratzinger, *Principles of Catholic Theology*, 47.
[20] Ratzinger, *Principles of Catholic Theology*, 32; Ratzinger, *Behold the Pierced One*, 105–106; Ratzinger, *Called to Communion*, 23.
[21] Ratzinger, *Principles of Catholic Theology*, 29–31.
[22] "Theology is a specifically Christian phenomenon which follows from the structure of faith. . . . It is preceded by a Word which … has been granted … as a gift. . . . Theology is pondering what God has said and thought before us." Ratzinger, *The Nature and Mission of Theology*, 103–104. "To perceive the meaning of this Word, to understand this Word—that is the ultimate basis of theology. . . ." Joseph Cardinal Ratzinger, *Pilgrim Fellowship of Faith: The Church as Communion*, trans. Henry Taylor (San Francisco: Ignatius, 2005), 32; Ratzinger, *Principles of Catholic Theology*, 325.

We "do" theology, in the first place, because we believe in—and we love—the God who has shown His face to us in Jesus Christ. Theology is faith seeking better understanding of the One who reveals Himself as love. It becomes an "imperative" of the faith because there is an innate human desire to seek the truth and the most intimate knowledge possible of the One we love. Listen, again, to Pope Benedict:

> Christian faith can say of itself, I have found love. Yet love for Christ and of one's neighbor for Christ's sake can enjoy stability and consistency only if its deepest motivation is love for the truth. This adds a new aspect to the missionary element: real love of neighbor also desires to give him the deepest thing man needs, namely, knowledge and truth.[23]

We see, then, that theology for Benedict is far from a private affair. Theology's desire to know and love God is always ordered to the Church's missionary proclamation of the saving Word—"to tell man who he is and ... to disclose to him the truth about himself, that is, what he can base his life on and what he can die for."[24]

In Benedict's understanding, there is an original and inner dynamism that orients theology to proclamation and to teaching. This does not reduce theology to apologetics or catechetics. Not in the least. Instead, Benedict sees a missionary impulse issuing from the very experience of Christian faith. Faith, because it possesses the truth about

---

[23] Ratzinger, *The Nature and Mission of Theology*, 27.
[24] Ibid., 63–64.

human history and human happiness, must necessarily express itself in proclamation and catechesis so that others may share in the truth.

If the activity of theology flows from the inner structure of Christian faith, its content and methodology issue in a similar way from the inner structure of revelation. Benedict takes up a distinction first drawn by Aristotle and later adopted by pseudo-Dionysius and Bonaventure. It's the distinction between *theology* proper, that is, the words of God, and the *study of theology*, that is, our efforts to understand the divine discourse.[25]

He sees Sacred Scripture as theology in its original and pure form, because it is "the discourse of God rendered in human words … it does not just speak of him but *is* his own speech. It lets God himself speak." He accepts the traditional Catholic notion of inspiration, of Scripture's twofold authorship, divine and human authorship. But he draws out a deeper implication, namely that the human authors of Scripture are the original theologians—"they are 'theologoi,' those through whom God … as the Word that speaks itself, enters into history."[26]

This fact of revelation has great significance for him: "the Bible becomes the model of all theology," and the authors of Sacred Scripture become "the norm of the theologian, who accomplishes his task properly only to the extent that he makes God himself his subject." This in turn leads to perhaps his most daring and fruitful assertion of theological principle. Listen closely, because he chooses every word carefully and doesn't waste a syllable:

---

[25] Ratzinger, *Principles of Catholic Theology*, 320–322.
[26] Ibid., 321.

[T]heology is a spiritual science. The normative theologians are the authors of Holy Scripture. This statement is valid not only with reference to the objective written document they left behind but also with reference to their manner of speaking, in which it is God himself who speaks.[27]

Theology is a spiritual science, and the normative theologians are the authors of Holy Scripture. For Benedict, that means that Scripture, and the human authors of Scripture, are meant to serve as the model—not only for how we should "do" theology, but also for what our theology should be about, and even how the findings of theological inquiry should be expressed.

Taking the New Testament authors as "normative" means, in the first place, that the theologian must be a person who has heard and believed the Word, professed that faith in the Church, and made personal assent to the standards and teachings of the Church in its sacramental and moral life. The New Testament authors were men of faith, and their written proclamation teaches us that the fullest knowledge of Christ is possible only for those who follow Him as disciples.[28] This leads Pope Benedict to an inevitable conclusion—that "theology presupposes faith. . . . There can be no theology without conversion."[29]

---

[27] Ibid., 320–322.

[28] See the biblical citations in Ratzinger, *On the Way to Jesus Christ*, 67. "[J]ust as we cannot learn to swim without water, so we cannot learn theology without the spiritual praxis in which it lives." Ratzinger, *Principles of Catholic Theology*, 323.

[29] Ratzinger, *The Nature and Mission of Theology*, 55, 57.

Following the New Testament writers, Benedict sees theology as essentially "about" Jesus Christ—about who He is, about the full meaning of the event of His Resurrection, and about how His presence remains in the world in His Church.[30] "All Christian theology, if it is to be true to its origin, must be first and foremost a theology of resurrection."[31] The primary data for theology become the words and deeds of Jesus as remembered and interpreted in the New Testament.[32]

Benedict then goes on to show us that the normative theologians of the New Testament were themselves in constant dialogue with the Old Testament texts. Indeed, Benedict sees the New Testament itself as a spiritual exegesis of the Old. "The New Testament is nothing other than an interpretation of 'the Law, the prophets, and the writings' found from or contained in the story of Jesus."[33] He notes that certain principles—"the internal unity of the Bible as a rule of interpretation, Christ as the meeting point of all the Old Testament pathways"—are the hallmarks of the New Testament authors' exegesis.[34]

The central event in salvation history, Christ's Resurrection, is both a mighty act of God and at the

---

[30] Ratzinger, *On the Way to Jesus Christ*, 76–77.

[31] Ratzinger, *Principles of Catholic Theology*, 184–185.

[32] "[T]he remembrance and retention of the words of Jesus and of the course of his life, especially his passion, were from the beginning an essential factor in the formation of Christian tradition and in the norms applied to it." Joseph Cardinal Ratzinger, *Dogma and Preaching*, trans. Matthew J. O'Connell (Chicago: Franciscan Herald, 1985), 4.

[33] Ratzinger, *Milestones: Memoirs, 1927–1977*, 53.

[34] Cardinal Joseph Ratzinger, "Preface," Pontifical Biblical Commission, *The Jewish People and their Sacred Scriptures in the Christian Bible* (Boston: Pauline Books and Media, 2003), 11–19, at 14.

same time a vindication of Jesus' interpretation of the Old Testament. Or, as Benedict puts it more pointedly, the Resurrection is "God's defense of Jesus against the official interpretation of the Old Testament as given by the competent Jewish authorities." By the Resurrection, God "proves," so to speak, that Jesus is the suffering servant, the divine Son, and the messiah from the line of David, as foretold by the prophets and the psalms. Of critical significance, in Benedict's mind, is the portrayal of Jesus as "the true lamb of sacrifice, the sacrifice in which the deepest meaning of all Old Testament liturgies is fulfilled." As we will see below, this has "essential significance for the Christian liturgy."[35]

As a final historical note, Benedict acknowledges that Jesus did not "invent" this way of reading the Scriptures. Already in the Old Testament, especially in the prophets and psalms, we find increasing anticipation of a messianic king who will be "the fulfilled image of the true Israel."[36] Nonetheless, Jesus does claim to be the definitive interpreter of the Old Testament texts, and the New Testament authors employed certain interpretive methods, already present in rabbinic Judaism, to back up this claim. As we will see, the resulting original Christian pattern of reading the New Testament in light of the Old and the Old Testament in light of the New becomes normative for Benedict's biblical theology.[37]

---

[35] Ratzinger, *Dogma and Preaching*, 3–5.

[36] Joseph Cardinal Ratzinger, *The Meaning of Christian Brotherhood*, trans. W. A. Glen-Doeple (San Francisco: Ignatius, 1993), 48.

[37] "Jesus of Nazareth claimed to be the true heir to the Old Testament —'the Scriptures'—and to offer a true interpretation, which, admittedly, was not that of the schools, but came from the authority of the Author himself: 'He

For Benedict, the sacramental liturgy of the Church, the worship of the new covenant, is the goal and consummation of the biblical story. If everything in Scripture is ordered to the covenant that God wants to make with His creation, then everything in the Church is ordered to proclaiming that new covenant and initiating people into the covenant through the sacraments. So the mission of the Church is liturgical. Its identity and actions are defined by the Word revealed in history.[38] In a sense, Benedict says, the revelation of God is not "complete" without the response of the Church in the liturgy, the primary expression of the Tradition.[39]

---

taught them as one having authority, and not as the scribes' (Mark 1:22). The Emmaus narrative also expresses this claim: 'Beginning with Moses and all the prophets, he interpreted to them the things about himself in all the Scriptures' (Luke 24:27). The New Testament authors sought to ground this claim into details, in particular Matthew, but Paul as well, by using rabbinic methods of interpretation to show that the scribal interpretation led to Christ as the key to the 'Scriptures.' For the authors and founders of the New Testament, the Old Testament was simply 'the Scriptures': it was only later that the developing Church gradually formed a New Testament canon which was also Sacred Scripture, but in the sense that it still presupposed Israel's Bible to be such, the Bible read by the apostles and their disciples, and now called the Old Testament, which provided the interpretative key." Ratzinger, "Preface," *The Jewish People and their Sacred Scriptures in the Christian Bible*, 17.

[38] "The Church … is there so that the world may become a sphere for God's presence, the sphere of the covenant between God and men … in order that the covenant may come to be in which God freely gives his love and receives the response of love." Ratzinger, *Pilgrim Fellowship of Faith*, 288–289.

[39] "Christians know that God has spoken through man and that the human and historical factor is, therefore, part of the way God acts. That, too, is why *the Word of the Bible becomes complete only in that responsive word of the Church which we call Tradition.* That is why the accounts of the Last Supper in the Bible become a concrete reality only when they are appropriated by the Church in her celebration." Ratzinger, *The Spirit of the Liturgy*, 169. Emphasis added.

In all his writings, Benedict emphasizes the unity of the liturgy of the old covenant with the liturgy of the new covenant. The Mass, he says, "places us in continuity with Israel and the whole of salvation history."[40] The Eucharist is the fulfillment of all the liturgies of the old covenant. Israel's ritual worship was ordered to remembrance, memorial, and "renewal of the covenant."[41] Christian worship, too, becomes a remembrance of God's mighty works in history. And like Israel's worship, especially the Passover Haggadah, the Eucharist is both a remembrance of the past and a thanksgiving for God's continued presence among His people.[42]

Christian liturgy, he notes, follows the basic pattern of Old Testament covenant worship—a service that includes both the reading of the Word of God and the offering of sacrifice. Benedict sees this outline reflected also in Jesus' Easter appearance to His disciples on the road to Emmaus (Luke 24:25–31). Jesus read and interpreted the Scriptures in light of His Resurrection, and then He revealed Himself in the breaking of the bread.[43]

---

[40] Pope Benedict XVI, Homily, Eucharistic Celebration at Cologne-Marienfeld, Germany (August 21, 2005), in *L'Osservatore Romano*, Weekly Edition in English (August 24, 2005), 11–12.

[41] Ratzinger, *Many Religions, One Covenant*, 62–65.

[42] Joseph Cardinal Ratzinger, *God Is Near Us: The Eucharist, the Heart of Life*, ed. S. O. Horn and V. Pfnur, trans. Henry Taylor (San Francisco: Ignatius, 2003 [2001]), 48–49.

[43] "First we have the searching of the Scriptures, explained and made present by the risen Lord; their minds enlightened, the disciples are moved to invite the Lord to stay with them, and he responds by breaking the bread for his disciples, giving them his presence and then withdrawing again, sending them out as his messengers." Joseph Cardinal Ratzinger, *Feast of Faith: Approaches to a Theology of the Liturgy*, trans. Graham Harrison (San Francisco: Ignatius, 1986), 47.

Benedict acknowledges, as well, the important role Scripture plays in the celebration of the Mass. During the course of the Church's year, he says, the lectionary readings "enable man to go through the whole history of salvation in step with the rhythm of creation."[44] Through the Word that's read and prayed in the liturgy, we believers are slowly transformed into the persons that God intends us to be.[45] In the liturgy, Benedict notes, the Old Testament is read typologically, as it is in the pages of the New Testament. The Old is read as foreshadowing the New. Yet that's not all there is to our remembrance. Because the liturgy doesn't merely evoke, or represent, or commemorate. It does those things, yes—but, more importantly, it brings about a kind of communion with the events narrated in the sacred pages. The liturgy, in a sense, effects the events that it signifies.

Benedict notices how the New Testament's typological interpretation of the Old is often ordered to the sacramental liturgy—especially as regards the central sacraments of Baptism and the Eucharist. He also conveys a sense of the mystery of the Word as living and active, bringing about the very promises that it speaks of in the life of the believer. "Scripture alive in the living Church is also God's present power in the world today—a power which remains an inexhaustible source of hope throughout all generations."[46]

---

[44] Joseph Cardinal Ratzinger, *Co-Workers of the Truth: Meditations for Every Day of the Year*, ed. Irene Grass (San Francisco: Ignatius, 1992 [1990]), 2.

[45] Through the liturgy, "the language of our Mother [the Church] becomes ours; we learn to speak it along with her, so that gradually, her words on our lips become our words. We are given an anticipatory share in the Church's perennial dialogue of love with him who desired to be one flesh with her." Ratzinger, *Feast of Faith*, 30.

[46] Ratzinger, *A New Song for the Lord*, 52.

The Bible is the interpretive key to the liturgy. But the reverse is true as well. Both realities, Bible and liturgy, are mutually interpretive. Liturgy, for its part, is the privileged context in which the community hears the Word and receives its authentic interpretation. This was the pattern of Christ at Emmaus. "Beginning with Moses and all the prophets, he interpreted to them in all the scriptures the things concerning himself" (Luke 24:27). In the Mass, we still hear the New Testament readings as *interpreting* the Old Testament *in light of Christ.* And it is in the liturgy that the texts are "realized" or "actualized" as Scripture, as divine, salvific communications. This is the way Pope Benedict puts it:

> The liturgy is the true, living environment for the Bible … The Bible can be properly understood only in this living context within which it first emerged. The texts of the Bible, this great book of Christ, are not to be seen as the literary products of some scribes at their desks, but rather as the words of Christ himself delivered in the celebration of holy Mass. The scriptural texts are thoroughly imbued with the awe of divine worship resulting from the believer's interior attentiveness to the living voice of the present Lord.[47]

And Benedict uses this interpretive key on every aspect of the sacramental mysteries.

For example, when he writes of the Eucharist as sacrifice, Benedict again shows himself to be conversant with

---

[47] Ratzinger, "Introduction," Guardini, *The Lord*, xii. Emphasis added.

the range of contemporary scholarship on the continuities between Jewish and Christian worship. He is impressed, for instance, by the evident influence of the old covenant *todah* (the "thanksgiving sacrifice") upon the ritual of the early Church. In the *todah*, the Israelites gave thanks to God for their deliverance from some life-threatening situation.[48] In thanksgiving they offered a sacrifice of unleavened bread and wine, and shared the meal with family and friends, while they sang a new song to the Lord. Benedict finds eloquent fulfillment of all this in the Mass, in the Christian thanksgiving, the Eucharist.

He finds further foreshadowing in the Old Testament understanding of sacrifice, as it is expressed in the psalms and prophets. In offering His life on the cross, and in establishing the Eucharist as a perpetual memorial of that self-offering, Jesus fulfilled all that had gone before. And He revealed something essential. He revealed that *the worship God desires* is "the transformation of existence into thanksgiving,"[49]—we "give ourselves back to him" in love and thanksgiving. That's the *todah*—and, even more, it's the Eucharist. The bottom line is that Scripture and liturgy are interdependent. When we examine one without the other, we are working within a severely limited horizon. We are, theologically speaking, vision impaired.

Benedict puts it, again, in more technical terms when he writes:

---

[48] Ratzinger, *Feast of Faith*, 51–60. Benedict's discussion includes a long and appreciative review of the scholarship of Hartmut Gese.
[49] Ratzinger, *God Is Near Us, 48, 51*

There is another fundamental hermeneutical aspect in the reading and the interpretation of biblical testimony. The fact that I can, or can not, recognize a sacrifice in the Eucharist as our Lord instituted it, depends most essentially on the question of knowing what I understand by sacrifice, therefore on what is called pre-comprehension . . . . For the believing theologian, it is clear that scripture itself must teach him the essential definition of sacrifice, and that will come from a "canonical" reading of the Bible, in which the scripture is read in its unity and its dynamic movement, the different stages of which receive their final meaning from Christ, to whom this whole movement leads. By this same standard, the hermeneutic here presupposed is a hermeneutic of faith, found on faith's internal logic. Ought not the fact to be obvious? Without faith, Scripture itself is not Scripture, but rather an ill-assorted ensemble of bits of literature which cannot claim any normative significance today.[50]

Yet we need not think that way. Nor should we. Instead, Benedict proposes the Bible as an inexhaustible source of insight on the liturgy, just as the liturgy is the primary context in which the saving truth of Sacred Scripture is proclaimed and actualized. Not only are the climactic moments of salvation history typically tied to liturgical events (like the first Passover and Exodus); these saving deeds are then re-presented in every subsequent generation precisely through the medium of the liturgy.

---

[50] Joseph Cardinal Ratzinger, lecture delivered during the Journees liturgiques de Fontgombault, July 22-24 2001.

Let's look at the event that is, for Benedict, most exemplary of these principles. In the unity of the Last Supper and the crucifixion, he sees the true depth of the Bible as the saving Word of God. For Christ intended His saving death to be re-presented in the sacrificial offering of the Eucharist. Indeed, His action is perpetuated in the sacramental form of the Eucharist, by which Christ transforms death itself into a life-giving word and deed. Thus, the Gospel of Christ is the good news that love is stronger than death.

The sacred Word heard in the Mass, and the sacrificial offering of that Word on the cross, come together in the Church's Eucharistic Prayer. Here, too, Benedict explains the Christian liturgy in terms of Old Testament belief— belief in the creative power of the Word of God as both speech and deed.[51] As God's Word created the heavens and the earth, and as Jesus' word healed the sick and raised the dead, the divine Word spoken in the liturgy also possesses creative and transformative power.[52]

In Benedict's biblical theology, *liturgy* is the goal of creation and the goal of the human person. In the liturgy, salvation history achieves its purpose. Heaven and earth are

---

[51] "God reveals himself in history. He speaks to humankind, and the word he speaks has creative power. The Hebrew concept '*dabar*,' usually translated as 'word,' really conveys both the meaning of *word* and act. God says what he does and does what he says." Pope Benedict XVI, "Message to the Youth of the World on the Occasion of the 21st World Youth Day" (April 9, 2006), in *L'Osservatore Romano*, Weekly Edition in English (March 1, 2006), 3.

[52] In the liturgy, the scriptural word is truly "the Word of transformation, enabling us to participate in the 'hour' of Christ. . . . It is the Word of power which transforms the gifts of the earth in an entirely new way into God's gift of himself, and it draws us into this process of transformation." Homily, Eucharistic Celebration at Cologne-Marienfeld (August 21, 2005).

filled with God's glory. Each participant is swept up into the embrace of salvation, into the communion of God's eternal love. The communion that God has desired since before the foundation of the world—between heaven and earth, between the visible and invisible, between the divine and human—is revealed and effected in the liturgy.

Every celebration of the Eucharist on earth becomes "a cosmic liturgy. . . . an entry into the liturgy of heaven."[53] In the liturgy, the eschatological orientation of Scripture is actualized. As Benedict describes it: "In the celebration of the liturgy, the Church moves toward the Lord; liturgy is virtually this act of approaching his coming. In the liturgy the Lord is already anticipating his promised coming. Liturgy is anticipated *parousia*."[54]

Benedict observes that many people today have a *fundamental misunderstanding* about the nature of liturgy and the nature of the Church. And the misunderstanding comes from faulty interpretation of the Bible. For much of the last century it has been an interpretive commonplace that the New Testament writers expected the imminent end of the world and return of Christ. Remarkably, this is

---

[53] Ratzinger, *The Spirit of the Liturgy*, 70.

[54] Ratzinger, *A New Song for the Lord*, 129. "Christian liturgy is never just an event organized by a particular group or set of people or even by a particular local Church. Mankind's movement toward Christ meets Christ's movement toward men. He wants to unite mankind and bring about the one Church, the one divine assembly, of all men . . . the communion of all who worship in spirit and in truth. . . . Christian liturgy is a liturgy of promise fulfilled, of a quest, the religious quest of human history, reaching its goal. But it remains a liturgy of hope. . . . Christian liturgy is liturgy on the way, a liturgy of pilgrimage toward the transfiguration of the world, which will only take place when God is 'all in all.'" Ratzinger, *The Spirit of the Liturgy*, 49–50.

one interpretation that both historical critics and funda-
mentalists hold in common. And it has led many scholars
to a troubling conclusion. As Benedict puts it, they conclude that "in his ideas about time Jesus was mistaken ...
[and] that Jesus' message is intrinsically incapable of being
appropriated by us."[55]

Indeed, he notes the methodological deficiency that
stems from an unwillingness to search out the meaning
of biblical texts in view of the liturgy and living Tradition
of the Church. He notes how this has caused exegetes to
ignore or downplay the fact that eschatological expressions
like *parousia* and *maranatha* properly "belong in the context of early Christian eucharistic celebration."[56]

Here again, Benedict builds his argument on solid linguistic and historical critical grounds. He agrees that the
normative theologians who authored the New Testament
expected a glorious coming or *parousia* of Christ. But, he
adds, it is clear from their language and contexts that this
parousia was anticipated, and in some way experienced,
in every celebration of the Eucharist. Listen closely to his
reasoned conclusion:

> The cosmic imagery of the New Testament cannot be
> used as a source for the description of a future chain of
> cosmic events. All attempts of this kind are misplaced.

---

[55] Joseph Cardinal Ratzinger, *Eschatology: Death and Eternal Life*, trans.
Michael Waldstein (Washington, D.C.: Catholic University of America Press,
2007), 271. On parousia (translated "coming" in Mt 24:27 and "presence" in
2 Cor 10:10 and Phil 2:12), see Scott Hahn, *Letter and Spirit: From Written
Text to Living Word in the Liturgy* (New York: Doubleday, 2006), 104–121.
[56] Ratzinger, *Eschatology*, 6, 202–203.; For Benedict's critique, see *Eschatology*,
35–45, 271–272. For the Aramaic expression, maranatha ("Our Lord,
come!"), see 1 Cor 16:22; Rev 22:20.

Instead, these texts form part of a description of the mystery of the *parousia* in the language of liturgical tradition. The New Testament conceals and reveals the unspeakable coming of Christ, using language borrowed from that sphere which is graciously enabled to express in this world the point of contact with God. The *parousia* is the highest intensification and fulfillment of the liturgy. And the liturgy is *parousia*, a *parousia*-like event taking place in our midst. . . . Every Eucharist is *parousia*, the Lord's coming, and yet the Eucharist is even more truly the tensed yearning that he would reveal his hidden glory. . . . In touching the risen Jesus, the Church makes contact with the *parousia* of the Lord.[57]

Benedict's biblical theology opens up fresh new possibilities for the study of Sacred Scripture and the practice of theology. What we see in his writings are "the essential elements for a synthesis between historical method and theological hermeneutics." And he himself has said that this synthesis can be found in the official teaching of the Church, as expressed in *Dei Verbum*.[58]

This synthesis promises us a way of reading Scripture authentically as it was written—as a divine, living Word spoken in history to the Church, a Word whose meaning is understood within the broad unity of the Church's experience of the faith, an experience that includes liturgy and dogma, and is not limited to the expectations and contexts of a text's original audience. Benedict goes so far as to

---

[57] Ratzinger, *Eschatology*, 202–204.
[58] Joseph Cardinal Ratzinger, *Schriftauslegung im Widerstreit*. Quaestiones Disputatae 117 (Freiburg: Herder, 1989), 20–21.

promise us theologians that this way of reading in continuity with Church's Tradition "increases the excitement and fecundity of inquiry."[59] You can hear the enthusiasm in his own words:

> [H]ow exciting exegesis becomes when it dares to read the Bible as a unified whole. If the Bible originates from the one subject formed by the people of God and, through it, from the divine subject himself, then it speaks of the present. If this is so, moreover, even what we know about the diversity of its underlying historical constellations yields its harvest; there is a unity to be discovered in this diversity, and diversity appears as the wealth of unity. This opens up a wide field of action both to historical research and to its hypotheses, with the sole limit that it may not destroy the unity of the whole, which is situated on another plane than what can be called the 'nuts and bolts' of the various texts. Unity is found on another plane, yet it belongs to the literary reality of the Bible itself.[60]

For the faithful theologian and exegete, the work of theology and exegesis assumes a place within the grand unity of God's plan as it is revealed in Scripture. Our task is all about the "divinization" of creation in the liturgical offering of the sacrifice of praise.[61]

> The unity of the person of Jesus, embracing man and God, prefigures that synthesis of man and world to which theology is meant to minister. It is my belief that

---

[59] Ratzinger, *The Nature and Mission of Theology*, 97.
[60] Ibid., 64–65.
[61] Ratzinger, *The Spirit of the Liturgy*, 28.

the beauty and necessity of the theologian's task could be made visible at this point. . . . But [the theologian] can only do this provided he himself enters that "laboratory" of unity and freedom ... where his own will is refashioned, where he allows himself to be expropriated and inserted into the divine will, where he advances toward that God-likeness through which the kingdom of God can come.[62]

Benedict bids the theologian and exegete to place himself in service to this divine plan. "We have to enter into a relationship of awe and obedience toward the Bible. . . . Historical-critical exegesis can be a wonderful means for a deeper understanding of the Bible if its instruments are used with that reverent love which seeks to know God's gift in the most exact and careful way possible."[63]

Hence, we understand Benedict's frequent exhortations concerning the need to retrieve the ancient practice of *lectio divina*, the loving contemplation of Scripture in which study is transformed into prayer.[64] Benedict presents us with a vision of a profound spiritual and scientific exegesis, a faith seeking understanding of the deepest mysteries of the cosmos, in conversation with the living God.

Benedict opens new avenues for exegetes and theologians alike, clergy and laity, professors and seminarians—one in which we see the profound unity of the Old and

---

[62] Ratzinger, *Behold the Pierced One*, 46.
[63] Ratzinger, *A New Song for the Lord*, 50.
[64] Pope Benedict XVI, "Reflection on the Opening of the Eleventh Ordinary General Assembly of the Synod of Bishops" (October, 3, 2005), in *L'Osservatore Romano*, Weekly Edition in English, October 12, 2005, 7.

New Testaments, Scripture and liturgy, Word and sacrament, theology and Church—a unity in service of God's plan, which is a participation in the mystery. In this way, we all find ourselves in the liturgy, under the authority of mystery, drawn together into the drama of divine redemption, not as mere spectators but as true participants.

Chapter Four

Scripture's Liturgical Sense

To my mind, one of the most notable achievements of twentieth-century biblical scholarship was the rediscovery of Scripture's *liturgical sense*. This achievement is rightly associated with the pioneering work of Oscar Cullman and Jean Danielou, who demonstrated that the biblical acts of God were intended to be carried on in the Church's sacramental liturgy. Their insights were reinforced by Henri de Lubac's study of medieval exegesis, and Yves Congar's historical and theological work on Tradition, which focused attention on the liturgy as the original and privileged locus of biblical interpretation.[1]

This essay appeared—with more extensive references and treatment of texts in their original languages—as "Worship in the Word: Toward a Liturgical Hermeneutic," in *Letter & Spirit*, vol. 1: *Reading Salvation: Word, Worship, and the Mysteries*, ed. Scott W. Hahn (Steubenville, OH: Emmaus Road, 2005), 101–136.

[1] See generally, Oscar Cullmann, *Early Christian Worship* (London, UK: SCM Press, 1962); Jean Danielou, *The Bible and the Liturgy* (Notre Dame, IN: University of Notre Dame Press, 1956) and Jean Danielou, "The Sacraments and the History of Salvation" from *The Liturgy and the Word of God* (Notre Dame, IN: University of Notre Dame Press, 1956); Yves Marie Joseph Congar, *Tradition and Traditions* (London: Burns & Oates, 1966) and Yves Marie Joseph Congar, *The Meaning of Tradition*, trans. A. N. Woodrow (San Francisco: Ignatius, 2004). "Let us not forget that Christian exegesis was born, first and foremost, in the office of the liturgy, regarding sacred reading that had to be commented upon. That is where it was developed." Henri de Lubac, *Medieval Exegesis* (Grand Rapids, MI: Eerdmans Publishing, 1998), 28.

This movement of recovery, which has continued among both Protestant and Catholic scholars,[2] is usually perceived as being in tension with historical and critical methodologies; but, in fact, these methods have also helped us to see that the Church's early cult and worship were decisive in the composition, content, and use of the scriptural texts.[3] As a result of these developments, we now have greater insight into the original purposes of the biblical authors and the ecclesial communities in which these texts were passed on. We can now appreciate that there is always a living and dynamic relationship between *Scripture*, the inspired Word of God in the Old and New Testaments, and *liturgy*, the sacrificial worship and public ritual of God's covenant people.[4]

---

[2] See Van Olst, *The Bible and The Liturgy*, trans. John Vriend (Grand Rapids, MI: Eerdmans Publishing, 1991); Hughes Oliphant Old, *The Reading and Preaching of the Scriptures in the Christian Church* (Grand Rapids, MI: Eerdmans Publishing, 2004); Cipriano Vagaggini, *Theological Dimensions of the Liturgy*, trans. Leonard J. Doyle and W. A. Jurgens (Collegeville, MN: Liturgical Press, 1976); Ratzinger, *The Spirit of the Liturgy*; Jean Corbon, *The Wellspring of Worship*, trans. Matthew J. O'Connell (San Francisco: Ignatius, 2005).

[3] For instance, source criticism, in moving from hypotheses about original documentary sources, discerns tradition, history and liturgical usage underlying biblical texts. Form criticism has also distinguished a variety of liturgical forms such as hymns and prayers, among kerygmatic, catechetical, and other forms. Redaction criticism, as well, has focused attention on how the historical situations of the various worshipping communities—the second Temple, the Johannine, and so forth—influenced the final shaping of the texts.

[4] Since "liturgy" means different things to different readers, depending in large part upon denominational background and worship experience, let me clarify that I am following the understanding of liturgy found in ancient Jewish and Christian sources, primarily the Bible; that is to say, I am considering liturgy as sacrificial worship and public ritual in the context of a divine-human covenant relationship.

Recognition of this vital relationship has important implications for the study of Scripture. Indeed, in this paper I will show how the rediscovery of Scripture's liturgical sense points to a new, *liturgical hermeneutic.* Such an interpretive approach leads us to conclude that Scripture is not solely text and liturgy is not solely ritual, even though the one exists as text and the other exists as ritual. As we can now see, liturgy is where the written text functions as Scripture, as the living Word of God. The liturgy emerges as the proper—though not exclusive—setting for reading and interpreting Scripture and for actualizing its saving truths.

I begin by showing how study of the *canon* and *covenant* has illuminated both the cultic *content* and *context* of the Bible. This in turn helps us to see what I call the *formal and material unity of Scripture and liturgy*—that Scripture exists *for* liturgy and, in large part, is *about* liturgy. This formal and material unity, I propose, invites us to make a fresh, *liturgical reading* of the integral text of the canonical Scriptures. As I hope to demonstrate, such a reading discloses a *liturgical trajectory* and *liturgical teleology* in the canonical narrative. This liturgical trajectory and teleology in turn suggests three broad principles of theological exegesis—the *divine economy, typology,* and *mystagogy.* I propose that these principles, which emerge from an integral reading of the canonical text, help us to lay the foundations for a new, *liturgical hermeneutic.*[5]

---

[5] These propositions are developed in Hahn, *Letter and Spirit,* vol. 1. For this approach see Ratzinger: "Since the inner unity of the books of the New Testament, and of the two testaments, can only be seen in light of faith's interpretation, where this is lacking, people are forever separating out new

The Liturgical Content and Context of Scripture
The Formal and Material Unity of Canon and Cult

The recovery of Scripture's liturgical sense by Cullman, Danielou, and others, dovetails with two critical findings of modern biblical scholarship: first, the recognition that Scripture's final canonical shape is essential for determining the meaning and purpose of individual passages and books and, secondly, the identification of covenant as Scripture's keynote narrative theme. Together, these findings have helped us to see a unity between Scripture and liturgy that is both formal and material. Their unity is *formal* in that Scripture was canonized for the sake of liturgy, and the canon itself derived from liturgical tradition. Their unity is *material* in that the content of Scripture is heavily liturgical.

Details about the origins of the *canon* as a definitive collection of sacred writings expressing the faith, worship, and instruction of the believing community remain elusive and are still debated.[6] However, there is increasing recognition that the motives for establishing the canon were

---

components and discovering contradictions in the sources. . . . *From a purely scientific point of view, the legitimacy of an interpretation depends on its power to explain things.* In other words, the less it needs to interfere with the sources, the more it respects the corpus as given and is able to show it to be intelligible from within, by its own logic, the more apposite such an interpretation is. Conversely, the more it interferes with the sources, the more it feels obliged to excise and throw doubt on things found there, the more alien to the subject it is. To that extent, *its explanatory power is also its ability to maintain the inner unity of the corpus in question.* It involves the ability to unify, to achieve a synthesis, which is the reverse of superficial harmonization. Indeed, only faith's hermeneutic is sufficient to measure up to these criteria." Ratzinger, *Behold the Pierced One*, 44–45. Emphasis mine.

[6] See generally, *The Canon Debate*, eds. Lee Martin McDonald and James A. Sanders (Peabody, MA: Hendrickson Publishers, 2002); Brevard Childs, "The Canon in Recent Biblical Studies: Reflections on an Era," in *Pro Ecclesia Pro: A Journal of Catholic and Evangelical Theology*, winter 2005, vol. XIV, no. 1.

largely cultic and that cultic use was an important factor in determining which Scriptures were to be included in the canon. Put simply, the canon was drawn up to establish which books would be read when the community gathered for worship, and the books included in the canon were those that were already being read in the Church's liturgy.[7]

The importance of liturgical use in the origins of the canon is not a new idea.[8] It has long been recognized, for instance, that what became canonical writings originated as

---

[7] In considering the contributions of Childs, Sanders has written: "That which is canon comes to us from ancient communities of faith, not just from individuals. … [T]he whole of the Bible, the sum as well as all its parts, comes to us out of the liturgical and instructional life of early believing communities." James A. Sanders, *From Sacred Story to Sacred Text* (Eugene, OR: Wipf & Stock Publishers, 2000), 162. Disputing another leading theory concerning the formation of the Hebrew biblical canon, McDonald states: "Acceptance into a collection of sacred scriptures did not have so much to do with a notion about the cessation of prophecy as with use in Israel's liturgy, or worship and instruction, over a long period of time." Lee Martin McDonald, *The Formation of the Christian Biblical Canon* (Peabody, MA: Hendrickson Publishers, 1995), 53. Bruce finds similar imperatives behind the formation of the New Testament canon: "When the canon was 'closed' in due course by competent authority, this simply meant that official recognition was given to the situation already obtaining in the practice of the worshipping community." Frederick Fyvie Bruce, *The Canon of Scripture* (Downers Grove, IL: InterVarsity Press, 1988), 42. Of the New Testament canon, Ferguson writes: "Distinctive worship practices also served as preconditions for a canon of Scripture. The Eucharist involved the remembrance of the passion of Christ and particularly the institution narrative. Prayers and confessional statements were grounded in the teachings of Jesus and the proclamation of his apostles. Christian materials were read in the assemblies from quite early (Mk. 13:14; Rev. 1:3). The Church did not have to wait until the end of the second century (and certainly not the fourth century) to know what books to read in church." Everett Ferguson, "Factors Leading to the Selection and Closure of the New Testament Canon," in *The Canon Debate*, eds. L. M. McDonald and J. A. Sanders, 296.

[8] "Many of the component parts of the New Testament were forged in the flame of corporate worship, and … this has left its stamp on its whole vocabulary." Charles Francis Digby Moule, *The Birth of the New Testament* (New York: Harper & Row, 1981), 20, cf. 33.

oral accounts of God's redemptive interventions in history recited in cultic settings and accompanied by ritual actions. This is true for both the Old and New Testament canons.[9] In each, we have testimony of authoritative scriptural texts being read in the worshipping assembly (Ex. 24:7; Deut. 31:9–13; Rev. 1:3; 1 Tim. 4:13). And textual analysis and form criticism have helped us to also see the profound shaping influence of liturgical use on the composition and final form of individual texts.[10] Broadly speaking, we can say that inasmuch as the exodus was the foundational narrative recalled and celebrated in Israel's liturgy, the "new Exodus" of Christ's death, Resurrection, and Ascension was the "subject" of the texts heard in the Church's eucharistic liturgy.

---

[9] See the early and important work of Gunnar Östborn, *Cult and Canon: A Study in the Canonization of the Old Testament* (Uppsala and Wiesbaden: A.-B. Lundequistska Bokhandeln and Otto Harrassowitz, 1950), especially ch. 5: "The Canon as Cultic Representation." See also, Artur Weiser, *The Old Testament: Its Formation and Development*, trans. Dorothea Barton (New York: Association Press, 1961): "The reading aloud of the written word in the cult gave a natural impetus to the collection of the Old Testament as sacred writings. Here is the real setting (*Sitz im Leben*) for the Old Testament as holy Scripture." Cf. Richard C. Leonard, "The Origin of Canonicity in the Old Testament" (Ph. D. dissertation, Boston University, 1972).

[10] Andrew McGowan, "'Is There a Liturgical Text in this Gospel?': The Institution Narratives and Their Early Interpretive Communities," from *Journal of Biblical Literature* 118 (1999); M. D. Goulder, *The Evangelists' Calendar: A Lectionary Explanation of the Development of Scripture* (London: SPCK, 1978); Willard M. Swartley, *Israel's Scripture Traditions and the Synoptic Gospels: Story Shaping Story* (Peabody, MA: Hendrickson, 1994); David Daube, "The Earliest Structure of the Gospels" from *New Testament Judaism: Collected Works of David Daube*, vol. 2, ed. Calum Carmichael (Berkeley, CA: University of California, 2000) 329–342.

Covenant and Cult

If the cultic worship of the Jewish and Christian communities gave rise to the canon, it is because that worship itself is a response to God's redemptive initiatives. In particular, the worship of Israel and the Church is a response to God's covenants. The unity that scholars have perceived between cult and canon is established and constituted by the covenant. Again, this is true for both the Hebrew biblical canon and the Christian Bible.

For both Israel and the Church, the Scriptures and the liturgical traditions of worship emerge as a single, inseparable response to God's redemptive initiative expressed in His offering of a covenant to His people. For Israel, the covenant at Sinai is foundational. For the Church, the "new covenant" made in the blood of Christ (Lk. 22:20) is foundational.[11] Indeed, it is instructive that *kanon* was not originally the word applied to the list of biblical books. Eusebius, writing in the early fourth century, rather spoke of the Scriptures as *endiathekai*—"encovenanted" or "contained in the covenant."[12]

---

[11] It is perhaps interesting to note that the exegesis of Pope Benedict XVI, sees a profound unity between the covenant at Sinai and the new covenant, a unity that reflects the inner continuity of the salvation history told in the canonical text: "With regard to the issue of the nature of the covenant, it is important to note that the Last Supper sees itself as making a covenant: it is the prolongation of the Sinai covenant, which is not abrogated, but renewed. Here renewal of the covenant, which from earliest times was doubtless an essential element of Israel's liturgy, attains its highest form possible." Ratzinger, *Many Religions, One Covenant*, 62.

[12] See McDonald and Sanders, *The Canon Debate*, 295–320, 432. On these themes, see also, Dennis J. McCarthy, *Institution and Narrative: Collected Essays* (Rome: Biblical Institute Press, 1985).

It is not surprising that many scholars have recognized the "covenant" as the recurrent and theologically significant theme in the canonical text. The vast literature on this topic cannot be rehearsed here.[13] Two things are important for our purposes: first, the finding that God's covenants with humanity form the narrative structure and dramatic content of the Bible;[14] secondly, the conclusion that the biblical covenants are initiated to form kinship or familial bonds between God and His people or family;[15] and, thirdly, that covenant-making is a cultic, liturgical act, as much as a legal and ethical one. This last point has not been well-studied. But it is crucial to see the unity of Scripture and liturgy in the establishment, renewal, and maintenance of God's covenant relationship with His people. Again, simply put, for both Christians and Jews, the scriptural texts

---

[13] For a review of the relevant themes and literature, see Scott Hahn, "Kinship by Covenant: A Biblical Theological Analysis of Covenant Types and Texts in the Old and New Testaments" (Ph.D. Dissertation, Marquette University, 1995) and "Covenant in the Old and New Testaments: Some Current Research (1994–2004)" in *Currents in Biblical Research* (April 2005, vol. 3, no. 2), 263–292.

[14] This is a finding that cuts across confessional lines. "The content and meaning of Scripture was God's covenant plan, finally realized in Jesus Christ (in his transitus) and in the Church." Congar, *Tradition and Traditions*, 68–69. See also Alan Segal, *Rebecca's Children: Judaism and Christianity in the Roman World* (Harvard University Press, 1986), 4; Nicholas Thomas Wright, *Christian Origins and the Question of God* (Minneapolis: Fortress Press, 2003), 260, 262. See also, "The Correlation of the Concepts of Canon and Covenant," in *New Perspectives on the Old Testament*, ed. J. B. Payne (Waco: Word Books, 1971), 265–279.

[15] See for example Ps 2:7; 2 Sam 8:14; Lev 26:12; Deut 32:6, 8, 18–19; Jer 30:22; Ezek 36:28; Hos 11:1; Gal 4:5–7; 1 Jn 3:2. Frank Moore Cross, "Kinship and Covenant in Ancient Israel," chap. 1 in *From Epic to Canon: History and Literature in Ancient Israel* (Baltimore: The Johns Hopkins University Press, 2000); Meredith G. Kline, *By Oath Consigned: A Reinterpretation of the Covenant Signs of Circumcision* (Grand Rapids: Eerdmans Publishing, 1968).

were originally enacted in the liturgy for the purposes of remembering and ritualizing the divine saving events, and renewing the people's covenant relationship with God.[16]

This helps to explain another seldom noticed fact: The books of the new and old covenants are heavily liturgical in content. This is what I mean in describing a *material unity* between Scripture and liturgy—the Bible in many ways is *about* liturgy. Much of the Pentateuch is concerned with ritual and sacrificial regulations; significant portions of the wisdom, historical, and prophetic books take up questions of ritual and worship. The New Testament, too, is filled with material related to the sacramental liturgy. The Gospel of John, for instance, unfolds as a kind of "sacramentary" in the context of the Jewish lectionary calendar; the Letter to the Hebrews and the Book of Revelation contain sustained meditations on the meaning of the Christian liturgy; and

---

[16] Very few commentators have recognized what Vanhoye has identified as the essential relationship between liturgical cult and covenant in the Bible: "The value of a covenant depends directly on the act of worship which establishes it. A defective liturgy cannot bring about a valid covenant. . . . The reason for this is easily understood. The establishment of a covenant between two parties who are distant from each other can only be accomplished by an act of mediation and, when it is a question of mankind and God, the mediation has of necessity to be conducted through the cult." Albert Vanhoye, *Old Testament Priests and the New Priest: According to the New Testament*, trans. J. Bernard Orchard (Petersham, MA: St. Bede's Publications, 1986) 181–182. Levenson, too, has seen this. "The renewal of the covenant was a central aspect of Israel's worship in biblical times." The purpose of liturgy, he adds, is "to actualize the past so that [each] new generation will become the Israel of the classic covenant relationship." Jon D. Levenson, *Sinai and Zion: An Entry into the Jewish Bible* (New York: Harper & Row, 1987) 80–81. See also, Menaham Haran, "The Berît 'Covenant': Its Nature and Ceremonial Background," in *Tehillah le-Moshe: Biblical and Judaic Studies in Honor of Moshe Greenberg*, eds. M. Gogan, B. L. Eichler, and J. H. Tigay (Winona Lake, IN.: Eisenbrauns, 1997), 203–219; Roland J. Faley, *Bonding with God: A Reflective Study of Biblical Covenant* (Mahwah, NJ: Paulist Press, 1997).

the letters of Paul and Peter are animated by liturgical and cultic concerns. Often it is liturgy, or the culpable neglect of liturgy, that drives the biblical drama. Also, though this topic has not been well-studied, liturgy appears at the most significant junctures of the salvation history recorded in the canonical Scriptures.[17]

Insofar, then, as the canon was established for use in the liturgy, and inasmuch as its content is "about" liturgy, it follows that we must engage Scripture *liturgically* if we are to interpret these texts according to the authors' original intentions and the life-situation of the believing community in which these texts were handed on. In what follows, I want to begin this process of engagement. Through canonical analysis, I want to offer a reading of the "meta-narrative" of Scripture, focusing on liturgy—what it is and how it functions in the Bible's grand "story."[18] Such a sketch must necessarily be broad brush. But by focusing on the central moments in the canonical narrative—creation, the exodus, the Davidic monarchy, and the new covenant—I believe we will see the familiar biblical outlines in a new light.

---

[17] See Scott Hahn, *Letter and Spirit*, especially ch. 3: "The Unities of Scripture and Liturgy." See also Raymond E. Brown, "The Johannine Sacramentary" in *New Testament Essays* (Milwaukee: Bruce Publishing Co., 1965); Augustine Pagolu, *The Religion of the Patriarchs* (New York: Continuum, 1998).

[18] See generally, Rolf Rendtorff, "Canonical Interpretation: A New Approach to Biblical Texts" in *Pro Ecclesia* 3 (1994); Craig G. Bartholomew and Michael W. Goheen, *The Drama of Scripture: Finding Our Place in the Biblical Story* (Ada, MI: Baker Academic, 2004); Kevin J. Vanhoozer, *First Theology: God, Scripture & Hermeneutics* (Downers Grove, IL: InterVarsity Press, 2002).

Reading Scripture Liturgically:
The Old Covenant Witness

Homo Liturgicus: Scripture's Liturgical Anthropology

I must begin by anticipating my conclusion. A liturgical reading of the canonical text discloses the Bible's *liturgical trajectory* and *liturgical teleology*. Put another way: as presented in the canonical narrative, there is a liturgical reason and purpose for the creation of the world and the human person and there is a liturgical "destiny" toward which creation and the human person journey in the pages of the canonical text. At each decisive stage in God's covenant relations with humanity, the divine-human relationship is expressed liturgically and sacrificially. The mighty acts of God in Scripture at every point climax in the liturgy, from the sacrificial offering of Noah following the flood to the institution of the Eucharist at the Last Supper. From the first page to the last, the canonical text presents us with a liturgical anthropology—the human person is *homo liturgicus*, created to glorify God through service, expressed as a sacrifice of praise.

This begins in the Bible's very first pages. In the liturgical hymn of Genesis 1, creation unfolds in a series of sevenfold movements, beginning with the first verse which is exactly seven words long in Hebrew, and proceeding with seven clearly defined creative speech acts of God ("Let there be …").[19] Linguistic and thematic parallels between

---

[19] Genesis 1 describes "a heavenly liturgy. With a severe and solemn rhythm the same expressions occur again and again throughout the whole chapter like a litany." Claus Westermann, *Der Schopfungsbericht vom Anfang der Bibel* (Stuttgart, 1960), quoted in Eugene R. Maly, "Israel—God's Liturgical People," in *Liturgy for the People: Essays in Honor of Gerhard Ellard, S. J. 1894–1963*, ed. William J. Leonard (Milwaukee: Bruce Publishing, 1963) 10–20 at 13.

the account of the primordial seven days and the later building of the tabernacle (Ex. 25–40)[20] have helped us to see the author's intent: to depict creation as the fashioning of a cosmic temple, which, like the later tabernacle and Temple, would be a meeting place for God and the human person made in His image and likeness.

In the second creation account in Genesis 2–3, the garden of Eden is described in highly symbolic terms as an earthly sanctuary—again with evident literary parallels to later sanctuaries, especially the inner sanctum of the Temple.[21] For our liturgical reading, the most important parallels are those that describe the terms of the relationship between God and man in the garden and in the sanctuary. God is described in "walking up and down" or "to and fro" in the garden (Gen. 3:8). The same Hebrew verb is used to characterize God's presence in the tabernacle (Lev. 26:12; Deut. 23:14; 2 Sam 7:6–7). The first man is described as placed in the garden to "till" or "serve" and to "keep" or "guard" it. The Hebrew verbs—'abodah and shamar—are only found together again in the Pentateuch to describe the liturgical service of the priests and Levites in the sanctuary (Num. 3:7–8; 8:26; 18:5–6).[22]

These literary clues suggest the biblical authors' intent to describe creation as a royal temple built by a heavenly king. The human person in these pages is intentionally

---

[20] Jon D. Levenson, "The Temple and the World" in *JR* 64 (1984), 285.
[21] Gordon J. Wenham, "Sanctuary Symbolism in the Garden of Eden Story," in *Proceedings of the Ninth World Congress of Jewish Studies* (Jerusalem, 1986), 19–25; Lawrence E. Stager, "Jerusalem and the Garden of Eden," *ERISR* 26 (1999), 183–94.
[22] Wenham, "Sanctuary Symbolism," 21.

portrayed as a royal firstborn and high-priestly figure, a kind of priest-king set to rule as vice-regent over the temple-kingdom of creation.[23]

The Priestly King of Genesis

This reading of Genesis is confirmed intertextually in the Old Testament and throughout the intertestamental and rabbinic literature. Perhaps the clearest inner-biblical reflection on the nature of the primal human is found in Ezekiel's famous lament over the King of Tyre (Ezek. 28:1–19).

Among numerous echoes of the original Eden account, Ezekiel describes the king as created in Eden, which is depicted as "the garden of God" and the "holy mountain of God"—that is, as a symbol of the site of the Temple (vv. 13, 14, 16). He "walks among the stones of fire" or burning coals (v. 14), which elsewhere are associated with the divine presence (Ezek. 1:3; Ps. 18:13). He is stamped with a "signet of perfection" or "of resemblance" (v. 12)—a symbol elsewhere associated with royal likeness and authority (Gen. 41:42; Hag. 2:23; Jer. 22:24–25).

As the king's creation is described in Adamic and priestly terms, so his sin is characterized as a form of sacrilege and profanation punished by exile and "deconsecration." The king's sin, like Adam's, is grasping after divinity—wanting to be "like a god." This becomes the refrain of Ezekiel's indictment (cf. Gen. 3:5, 22; Ezek. 28:2, 6, 9). Driven by cherubim he is cast from God's presence as a "profane

---

[23] Dexter E. Callender, *Adam in Myth and History: Ancient Israelite Perspectives on the Primal Human* (Winona Lake, IN: Eisenbrauns, 2000), 29.

thing" who has desecrated God's sanctuaries (Ezek. 28:16, 18; cf. Gen. 3:23–24).

This passage of Ezekiel suggests that already within the Old Testament there was a traditional understanding of the human person as created in relationship with God and endowed with an identity that is at once royal and priestly, filial and liturgical.[24] The terms of the human relationship with God are ordered by the covenant of the Sabbath established on the seventh day. The first of God's mighty works then, the creation of the world, has a liturgical climax—the divine and human "rest" of the seventh day.[25] This will become clearer further on in the Pentateuch, as we see with Moses' building of the tabernacle and God's giving of the Sabbath ordinances.

The Priestly People of the Exodus

These creation themes—man as made for worship in a covenant relationship as God's royal and priestly firstborn—are made explicit in the canonical account of the

---

[24] Ibid., 132.

[25] The term "covenant," of course, is not used in the creation account. However, that creation is ordered to the covenant is everywhere implied. See Robert Murray, *The Cosmic Covenant: Biblical Themes of Justice, Peace and the Integrity* (Piscataway, NJ: Gorgias Press, 2006). The sabbath was seen as a sign of God's covenant oath with the first man and woman in the rabbinic and intertestamental literature. See, for instance, the midrashic *Sifre Deuteronomy*, the *Book of Jubilees* (36:7), and *1 Enoch* 69:15–27. See also Roland De Vaux, *Ancient Israel: Its Life and Institutions*, trans. John McHugh (Grand Rapids, MI: Eerdmans Publishing, 1997): "Creation is the first action in this history of salvation; once it was over, God stopped work, and he was then able to make a covenant with his creature. . . . The 'sign' of the covenant made at the dawn of creation is the observance of the sabbath by man (Ezek 20:12, 20)." Recent Catholic magisterial documents have referred to the sabbath of creation as "the first covenant." See John Paul II, *Dies Domini*; cf. *Catechism of the Catholic Church*, no. 288.

Exodus. As Adam was made in God's image and likeness, God identifies Israel as "my own people" (Ex. 3:7, 10, 12; 5:1; 6:5, 7) and "my son, my firstborn" (Ex. 4:22–23). And as Adam was made to worship, God's chosen people are liberated expressly for worship.

The early chapters of Exodus involve a play on the Hebrew word for "serve" or "work," the word that described the primeval vocation given to man (Gen. 2:15). The word is used four times to stress the cruel slavery ("hard service") inflicted upon the Israelites by the new Pharaoh (Ex. 1:13–14; see also 5:18; 14:5, 12). But the same word is also used to describe what God wants of the Israelites (Ex. 3:12; 4:22; 7:16; 9:1, 13; 10:3, 24–26). They are to serve, not as slave laborers but as a people that serves Him in prayer.[26] They are to "offer sacrifice" (Ex. 3:18; 5:3). Moses and Aaron are instructed to tell Pharaoh that God wants Israel to hold a religious "feast" or "festival" (Ex. 5:1; cf. Ex. 12:14; 23:16; 34:25).

Israel's vocation is most clearly stated in the preamble to the covenant at Sinai. There God calls Israel "a kingdom of priests and a holy nation" (Ex. 19:5–6).[27] Israel is to be corporately what Adam was created to be individually— the firstborn of a new humanity, a liturgical people that will dwell with God in a relationship of filial obedience and worship.

The covenant at Sinai is ratified by liturgical actions— the reading of the book of the law, the profession of fidelity

---

[26] Note the use of *'abodah* (to describe the priestly liturgical service offered to God in the tabernacle (Num 3:7–8; 4:23; 7:5; 16:9).

[27] Jo Bailey Wells, *God's Holy People: A Theme in Biblical Theology* (New York: Continuum, 2000), 34–35.

sworn by the people, the offering of sacrifices, the sprin-
kling of "the blood of the covenant," and the meal eaten
in the presence of God (see Ex. 24:1–9). Much of the Law,
in fact, consists of regulations regarding how God is to
be rightly worshipped—the design of the tabernacle and
furniture, the priestly vestments, the liturgical calendar of
festivals, and ceremonial rubrics of the sacrificial system.
In their worship, the Israelites celebrated their birth as a
people of God and rededicated themselves to their royal
and priestly vocation (Deut. 6:4–5).[28]

As creation was ordered to the Sabbath, the Exodus
is likewise ordered to a liturgical "end." The Exodus
was begun with a liturgical act—the celebration of the
Passover. And it "concludes" in the canonical text with the
construction of the tabernacle. The literary parallels with
the creation account suggest a close connection between
Sabbath, creation, covenant, and the dwelling that Israel is
instructed to build.[29] The plans for the dwelling are given
by God immediately after the liturgical ratification of the
Sinai covenant in Exodus 24. Moses' time on the mountain can be seen as a kind of "new creation"—the cloud of
divine presence covers the mountain for six days and on the
seventh Moses is called to enter the cloud and receive the
divine blueprint for the dwelling. God's instructions con-
sist of a series of seven commands that continue for seven
chapters and conclude with the ordinances for the seventh
day, the Sabbath (Ex. 31:12–17).

---

[28] Levenson, *Sinai and Zion*, 80–81.
[29] For these parallels, see Samuel Eugene Balentine, *The Torah's Vision of
Worship* (Minneapolis: Fortress Press, 1999), 136–41; Gary A. Anderson, *The
Genesis of Perfection* (Louisville, KY: Westminster John Knox Press, 2003),
200–02.

The making of the priestly vestments and the building of the tabernacle again recall the creation narrative. In both, the work is also done in seven stages, each punctuated with the words, "as the LORD commanded Moses." As God did, Moses beholds his handiwork, and blesses it (Ex. 39:43). As God "finished his work," so Moses "finished the work" (Gen. 2:1–2; Ex. 40:33). And as God rested on the seventh day, blessing and hallowing it, when Moses finished his work the divine presence filled the tabernacle (Ex. 40:34).

In the Israelites' work to build the tabernacle we glimpse what the royal and priestly service of the human person was meant to be about: God's sons and representatives were to rule in His name, according to His commands. Through their work they were to bring creation to its fulfillment, to complete God's work by making the world a home in which they dwell with Him and live as His people.[30]

All of creation is ordered to the covenant, this familial dwelling of God with His people. The Sabbath, as the sign of God's "perpetual covenant" (Ex. 31:16), is meant to be a living memorial of the original perfection and intention of God's creation—His desire to "rest" in communion with creation. The Sabbath orders human work to worship, labor to liturgy. The royal calling to subdue the earth finds its expression in the liturgical consecration of the earth's fruits to God. Through their worship on the Sabbath, God bestows His blessings on His people and makes them holy (Ex. 31:13).[31]

---

[30] See Anderson, *Genesis of Perfection*, 201–02.

[31] "The sabbath is the sign of the covenant between God and man; it sums up the inward essence of the covenant. . . . [C]reation exists to be a place for

As Israel is given an "Adamic" vocation, it experiences an Adamic fall from grace. And as the primeval fall results in exile and deconsecration of the royal priestly figure, so too does Israel's worship the golden calf.[32] God calls the people "corrupted," using a Hebrew term (Ex. 32:7) found elsewhere to describe an animal too blemished to sacrifice or a priest unfit for service.[33] In defiling itself through ritual rebellion, Israel, like Adam, is rendered unfit for its divine vocation. It is interesting that the royal-priestly title of Exodus 19:6 is never again used to describe Israel in the Old Testament.

According to the biblical narrative, the apostasy results in the Levitical priesthood becoming the locus of the holiness that God intended for all Israel.[34] God's presence

---

the covenant that God wants to make with man. The goal of creation is the covenant, the love story of God and man. . . . If creation is meant to be a space for the covenant, the place where God and man meet one another, then it must be thought of as a space for worship. ... Now if worship, rightly understood, is the soul of the covenant, then it not only saves mankind but is also meant to draw the whole of reality into communion with God." Ratzinger, *The Spirit of the Liturgy*, 26–27.

[32] See Hahn, "Kinship by Covenant," 226–53.

[33] See also Lev 22:25, Mal 1:14; 2:8. "The point to notice here is that the people of Israel as a whole now have a moral defect that separates them from God. They cannot come to the sanctuary for they have rejected God, and thus have become like a defective animal or a disqualified priest, unable to come into God's presence." A. M. Rodriguez, "Sanctuary Theology in Exodus," in *Andrews University Seminary Studies 24* (1986), 139.

[34] John M. Scholer, *Proleptic Priests: Priesthood in the Epistle to the Hebrews* (New York: Continuum, 1991), 13–22. Although well beyond what I can do here, it is worth noting that the "liturgical reading" of Scripture helps us to understand why, by the Second Temple period in general, and in the Qumran material in particular, we have such an explicitly developed Adamic, high priestly theology. In other words, Israel's high priest is portrayed as a kind of "new Adam" who represents Israel, which in turn is seen as a kind of "new humanity" that exists for "liturgical" ends. See Crispin H. T. Fletcher-Louis,

remains among the people, but access is highly restricted and must be mediated by the Levites. A complex array of cultic laws were introduced for apparently penitential and pedagogical purposes—as mechanisms that will enable Israel to atone for its inevitable sins against the covenant and to teach them the true meaning of worship.[35]

The Priestly Kingdom of David

Creation was ordered to the Sabbath worship of the royal and priestly first couple. The Exodus was ordered to the establishment of Israel as a priestly people to offer service to God. The Exodus began with the Passover liturgy and culminated in the building of the tabernacle, and the liturgical celebration of God's presence filling the sacred space. The conquest of the land was ordered to the establishment of the priestly kingdom of David. And following the pattern of the Exodus, the conquest of the land began with the overthrow of Jericho by "liturgical" means—not by military engagement but by a liturgical procession led by the Ark of the Covenant and Israel's priests. Also, as the Exodus culminated in the erection of the tabernacle, so too, the conquest culminates in the construction of the Temple and the liturgical celebration of God's abiding presence.

The Davidic kingdom marks the fullest expression of the Bible's liturgical anthropology and teleology. In the dynasty

---

"Jesus and the High Priest," available at http://www.marquette.edu/maqom/jesus.pdf, and *All the Glory of Adam: Liturgical Anthropology in the Dead Sea Scrolls* (Boston: Brill, 2002).

[35] See the important contributions of Hartmut Gese on "The Law" and "The Atonement" in his *Essays on Biblical Theology* (Minneapolis: Augsburg, 1981), 60–116.

established by His covenant with David, God restates His divine will for the human person: to be a son of God, a priest, and a king.[36] The royal-priestly primogeniture granted to David's seed (2 Sam 7:14; Ps. 110:4; 89:26–27) is linked to the royal priesthood intended for Israel (Ex. 3:6–17; 4:22; 19:5–6). David is portrayed as a "new Melchizedek"—a priest and king who serves the most high God from his capital in Salem, that is, Jerusalem (cf. Gen. 14:18; Ps. 76:2; 110). David is shown taking actions that are at once cultic and political, military and liturgical. His first act, after establishing Jerusalem as capital of his kingdom, is to restore the Ark of the Covenant—the defining symbol of Israel's election and the site of God's living presence among the people during the wilderness period (Ex. 25:8–22; Josh. 3:8–11).

David's great concern for the Ark is central to the early drama of his reign, and the Ark's installation in the Temple marks the culmination of the Chronicler's account.[37] As the architectural expression of the Sinai covenant was the tabernacle, the architectural expression of the Davidic Kingdom was not a royal palace, but the Temple.

The building of the Temple is presented as a new creation. As creation takes seven days, the Temple takes seven years to build (1 Kings 6:38; Gen. 2:2). It is dedicated

---

[36] See the discussion in Hahn, "Kinship by Covenant," 359–60; see also Heinz Kruse, "David's Covenant" in *Vetus Testamentum* 35 (1985), 139–64; Jon Levenson, "The Davidic Covenant and its Modern Interpretations" in *Catholic Biblical Quarterly* 41 (1979), 205–19.

[37] See Christopher T. Begg, "The Ark in Chronicles," in *The Chronicler as Theologian* (New York: T&T Clark, 2003), 133–43.

during the seven-day Feast of Tabernacles (1 Kings 8:2) by a solemn prayer of Solomon structured around seven petitions (1 Kings 8:31–53).

In the Temple worship, the precise sacrificial system of the Mosaic cult continues, but there are new elements and accents. The kingdom's corporate worship takes the form of praise and thanksgiving. Many commentators have identified the centrality of songs of praise and songs of thanksgiving in the Temple liturgy. Many of the psalms of praise appear to have been written to accompany the offering of sacrifices in the Temple (Ps. 27:6; 54:6, 8; 141:2). This is true also for the "thanksgiving songs" organized by the Levites (Neh. 11:17; 12:8, 31).

David's own thanksgiving hymn (1 Chron. 16:7–36) is presented as a kind of paradigm for Israel's prayer. It is, in essence, a celebration of God's covenant in liturgical form. This hymn sets the tone and provides the content for the acts of worship and the theology of worship we find in the Psalter. God is praised and thanked in remembrance of His mighty works in creation and for his saving words and deeds in the life of Israel—the defining experience being that of the Exodus and the covenant.

The Sacrifice of Praise

Praise and thanksgiving, accompanied by sacrifice, is understood to be the only appropriate response to the God who has created Israel to be His own and rescued them from death.[38] This is seen most evocatively in the *todah* or

---

[38] J. Kenneth Kuntz, "Grounds for Praise: The Nature and Function of the Motive Clause in the Hymns of the Hebrew Psalter," in *Worship and the Hebrew Bible: Essays in Honor of John T. Willis*, ed. M. Patrick Graham and others (Sheffield UK: Sheffield Academic Press, 1999), 182–83.

thanksgiving psalms (for example, Ps. 18; 30; 32; 41; 66; 116; 118; 138). Composed to accompany the offering of a sacrificial meal of bread and meat in the Temple (Lev. 7:1–21), these are some of the highest expressions of the Old Testament's liturgical anthropology.[39]

In the *todah* psalms the experience of the individual believer is almost typologically compared to that of Israel's captivity and exodus experience. Typically these psalms begin with a confession of faith and a vow of praise and self-offering. There follows a lament concerning some life-threatening distress that had befallen the believer. Then the believer describes how God delivered him from death or Sheol (the netherworld) and brought him to sing God's praises in the Temple.[40] In these psalms, "life" is equated with worship and sacrifice in the presence of God in His Temple; "death" is seen as a sort of exile or captivity, to be cut off from God's presence, outside His Temple.[41]

We see in these psalms and in the prophetic literature a new and deepening understanding of the liturgical vocation of biblical man. In the prophets, this recognition of the inner truth of sacrifice often takes the form of denouncing the corruption of Israel's cult and worship (for example,

---

[39] "It can be said that the thank-offering constituted the cultic basis for the main bulk of the psalms. It not only represents the high point of human life, but in it life itself can be seen as overcoming the basic issue of death by God's deliverance into life." Gese, *Essays on Biblical Theology*, 131. On the spirituality of the *todah* and its influence on Christology, see Ratzinger, *The Spirit of the Liturgy*, 54–57.

[40] See Hermann Gunkel, *Introduction to Psalms: The Genres of the Religious Lyric of Israel*, trans. James D. Nogalski (Macon, GA: Mercer University Press, 1998), 199–221.

[41] Gary A. Anderson, "The Praise of God as a Cultic Event," in *Priesthood and Cult in Ancient Israel*, (Sheffield, UK: JSOT Press, 1991), 28.

Is. 1:10–13; 66:2–4; Jer. 7:21–24; Amos 4:4–5, 6b; Mic. 6:6–8; Hos. 6:6; Mal. 1:10, 13–14). Positively, worship comes to be seen as a sacrificial offering in thanksgiving for redemption, for deliverance from death. Praise is revealed as the sacrifice by which men and women are to glorify God (Ps. 50:14, 23; 141:2). God is portrayed as desiring that Israel serve Him—not with the blood of animals but with their whole hearts, aligning their will with His, making their whole lives a sacrifice of praise and thanksgiving (Ps. 40:6–8; 51:16–17).

With this profound understanding that they are called to a pure worship from the heart comes the recognition that no amount of ethical striving or moral reform can make them holy enough to serve their God. A new covenant is promised as a new Exodus and a new creation in which there will be a forgiveness of sins and a divine transformation of the heart (Jer. 31:31–34; 32:40; Ezek. 36:24–28).

In the vision of the prophets, the new Exodus will mark a renewal of Israel's vocation as the firstborn and teacher of the nations. Isaiah sees Israel fulfilling its ancient vocation as "priests of the LORD" (Is. 61:6), and the instrument of God's blessings for the nations (Is. 19:24). Isaiah foresees nations streaming to Zion to worship the Lord (Is. 2; see also Jer. 3:16–17)—including arch-foes Egypt and Assyria, which serve Israel's God and offer sacrifices and burnt offerings.[42]

---

[42] Christopher T. Begg, "The Peoples and the Worship of Yahweh in the Book of Isaiah," in *Worship and the Hebrew Bible*, eds. M. P. Graham and others (Sheffield, UK: Sheffield Academic Press, 1999); Ronald E. Clements, "A Light to the Nations: A Central Theme of the Book of Isaiah," in *Forming Prophetic Literature: Essays on Isaiah and the Twelve*, eds. James W. Watts and Paul R. House (New York: Continuum, 1996).

We see then, on the threshold of the New Testament, the promise that man's primal vocation will be renewed, that Israel will be gathered together with all nations at Zion to offer acceptable sacrifice to the God of Israel.

Reading Scripture Liturgically:
The New Covenant Witness

The New Genesis and the New Adam

In the New Testament Jesus and His Church are presented as the fulfillment of the promises and institutions of the old covenant.[43] The story of the Incarnation is told as a new creation. In Jesus there is a new beginning for the human race. He is explicitly called the new Adam (Rom. 5:12–20; 1 Cor. 15:45–49). In the early chapters of the Letter to the Hebrews—especially in the opening catena of seven Old Testament quotations—Jesus is described in terms of Adam's original royal, filial, and priestly vocation.[44] Here and throughout the Pauline corpus, it is understood that the human vocation was frustrated at the outset by Adam's sin.

It is impossible to put forward here a biblical-theological argument concerning the specific nature of Adam's sin.[45] However, I would suggest that Adam's disobedience was understood inner-biblically as having something to do

---

[43] For extensive bibliographies see Steven Moyise, *Old Testament in the New: An Introduction* (New York: Continuum, 2004).

[44] See William L. Lane, *Hebrews 1–8*, vol. 47a, *Word Biblical Commentary* (Nashville, TN: Thomas Nelson, 1991), 46–50.

[45] For recent theories, see James Barr, *The Garden of Eden and the Hope of Immortality* (Minneapolis: Fortress Press, 1993), 1–20; Sibley Towner, "Interpretations and Reinterpretations of the Fall," in *Biblical Scholarship: Its Impact on Theology and Proclamation*, ed. Francis A. Eigo (Villanova, PA: Villanova University Press), 53–85.

with a failure to offer himself—what we might call a failure of worship. His transgression of God's command betrays a broader abdication of his task of priestly service in the temple of creation.[46] In this sense, the story of the fall is truly the first chapter of the Bible, preparing the reader for Israel's history. That history unfolds according to the pattern of Eden: divine benediction is offered and accepted, only to be followed quite immediately by human profanation, resulting in punishment by exile from the land of God's presence.[47]

I do not want to reduce the history of sin in the Bible to a story of cultic failure. But I do want to suggest that a liturgical reading of Scripture enables us to better understand why Christ's "obedience" is so often cast in cultic, sacrificial, and priestly terms. The identification of Christ's redemptive work with cultic sacrifice is especially strong in those passages that most scholars agree represent christological hymns used in early Christian worship.[48]

The hymn in Paul's letter to the Philippians (2:6–11)[49] underscores the dramatic reversal of Adam's sin. Unlike

---

[46] G.K. Beale, *The Temple and the Church's Mission: A Biblical Theology of the Dwelling Place of God* (Downers Grove, IL: InterVarsity, 2004), 69–70.

[47] "[T]he story of Adam and Eve in the J source shows a striking parallel to Israel's larger national story. We might say that the entire narrative of the Torah is in tersely summarized form. … Adam and Eve fall at the first and only command given to them. And like the nation Israel, the consequences of their disobedience is exile from a land of blessing." Anderson, *The Genesis of Perfection*, 207–08.

[48] For example, see the redemptive "blood" imagery in Rom 3:24–25; Eph 1:3–14; 2:13; Col 1:15–20; Heb 1:3; 1 Pet 1:18–21. On these hymns, see M. Hengel, "Hymns and Christology," in *Between Jesus and Paul* (London: SCM, 1983).

[49] James D. Martin, *Carmen Christi* (Cambridge: Cambridge University Press, 2005).

Adam, who was made in the image of God, Christ did not grasp at equality with God but, instead, offered His life in humility and obedience to God. In Hebrews, this obedience is compared to the liturgical act of high-priestly sacrifice (Heb. 9:11–28). As Israel's high priests would enter the sanctuary once a year to offer animal blood in atonement for the people's sins, Jesus enters the "true" sanctuary—"heaven itself" (Heb. 9:24)—to offer His own blood in sacrifice "to bear the sins of many" (Heb. 9:28).

By this priestly act, this offering of blood, Jesus does even more than atone for sin. He also reveals the true nature of sacrifice as intended by God from the beginning—man's offering of himself in filial obedience to the divine will. Hebrews explains this through a christological reading of Psalm 40, finding in it a prophecy of Christ's offering of His body on the cross (Heb. 10:5–10).

Christ's self-offering is the worship expected originally of Adam and again of Israel as God's firstborn, royal, and priestly people. His sacrifice marked the fulfillment of all that Israel's sacrificial system was intended to prepare and instruct Israel for—that through Israel all the nations of the world might learn to make a perfect offering of heart and will to God.[50]

The New Exodus

As the New Testament presents it, Jesus' sacrificial death brought about a new exodus—liberating God's people from slavery to sin and subjection to death, ending their exile

---

[50] Yves Congar, *The Mystery of the Temple, Or, The Manner of God's Presence to His Creatures,* trans. Reginald Frederick Trevett (Westminster, MD: Newman Press, 1962), 126, 141.

from God, gathering them and all peoples, and leading them into the promised land of the heavenly kingdom and the new Jerusalem.

This "new Exodus" theme is now widely recognized as a decisive and shaping factor in the New Testament.[51] It is now widely accepted that Jesus is presented as a "new Moses." His Passion and death are described as an "exodus" (*exodon*, Lk. 9:31) in a transfiguration scene filled with allusions to the theophanies of the wilderness period. And His death on the cross is described as a paschal sacrifice— that is, in terms of the liturgical sacrifice commanded by God to be offered on the night before Israel's Exodus (Jn. 1:29, 33; 19:14, 33, 36; 1 Pet. 1:19; 1 Cor. 5:7; Rev. 5:6, 9; 7:17; 14:1; 15:3).

This typological reading of a new Exodus and a new passover is hardly contested. It is also generally accepted that the New Testament writers present the sacraments of Baptism and the Eucharist as means by which Christian believers are joined to the new Exodus. Baptism is prefigured by the Israelites' passage through the Red Sea, the Eucharist prefigured by the manna and the water from the rock in the desert (1 Cor. 10:1–4; Jn. 6). As the first Exodus is preceded by the institution of a liturgical memorial, by which Israelites would annually celebrate their

---

[51] See most recently, Dale C. Allison, *The New Moses: A Matthean Typology* (Minneapolis: Fortress Press, 1994); Rikki E. Watts, *Isaiah's New Exodus in Mark* (Ada, MI: Baker Academic, 2001); David W. Pao, *Acts and the Isaianic New Exodus* (Ada, MI: Baker Academic, 2002); Sylvia C. Keesmaat, *Paul and His Story: (Re)interpreting the Exodus Tradition* (Sheffield, UK: Sheffield Academic Press, 1999).

establishment as a people of God, so too Christ institutes a memorial of His exodus sacrifice in the Eucharist inaugurated in the last supper with His disciples.

But a critical aspect of the typology has gone largely unnoticed in the literature—how the New Testament writers appropriate the Old Testament understanding of the *purpose* for the Exodus. As we saw, God's liberation of Israel was ordered to a very specific end—namely, the establishment of Israel as God's royal and priestly people destined to glorify Him among the nations.

Echoes of that exodus purpose are clearly heard in Zechariah's canticle at the outset of Luke's Gospel (1:67–79). In a song resounding with exodus imagery,[52] Zechariah sees the "goal" of Christ's exodus as precisely that of the first Exodus—to establish Israel as a holy and righteous people that worships in God's presence. Luke even employs here the specific term for the covenant "service" that God intended for Israel.[53]

In 1 Peter, we encounter a rich passage (1 Pet. 1:13–20; 2:1–10) in which the Exodus themes are applied to the newly baptized. They are told to "gird up the loins," as the Israelites did on the night of their flight (Ex. 12:11). Peter says they have been "ransomed" (1 Pet. 1:18), using the same word used to describe Israel's deliverance (Ex. 15:13), by the blood of a spotless unblemished lamb (Ex. 12:5).

---

[52] See the review of "scriptural metaphors derived from the exodus" in Joel B. Green, *The Gospel of Luke*, volume in *New International Commentary on the New Testament*, (Grand Rapids MI: Eerdmans Publishing, 1997), 110–20.
[53] See Deut 11:13. See David Mathewson, *A New Heaven and a New Earth* (New York: Continuum, 2993), 205–206. See also Joseph A. Fitzmyer, *The Gospel According to Luke I-IX* vol. 28, *The Anchor Bible* (New York: Doubleday, 1982), 1:385; Green, *The Gospel of Luke*, 117.

Their lives are described as a sojourning like that of Israel in the wilderness; they too are fed with spiritual food as the Israelites drank living water from the rock in the desert.

Finally, this passage culminates with the explicit declaration that the Church is the new Israel—"a chosen race, a royal priesthood, a holy nation." This direct quotation from the Septuagint translation of Exodus 19:6 is joined to a quote from an Isaianic new Exodus text that foresees the world-missionary dimension of Israel's royal and priestly vocation as "the people whom I formed for myself, *that they might announce my praise*" (1 Pet. 2:9–10; Is. 43:21).

The New Priestly Kingdom

Christ's new Exodus is ordered to the establishment of the priestly kingdom that God intended in the first Exodus. This understanding is enriched by another type found in the New Testament writings—that of the Church as the restored kingdom or house of David. Jesus is portrayed throughout the New Testament as the son of David anticipated in the Old Testament, a priest-king according to the order of Melchizedek.[54] The Church, heir of the royal priestly sonship of Israel, is said to participate in the heavenly high priesthood and royal sonship of Christ.

The redemptive work of Christ is both sacrificial and priestly. It brings about "purification from sins," Hebrews

---

[54] See Scott Hahn, "Kingdom and Church in Luke-Acts," in *Reading Luke*, eds. Craig G. Bartholomew and others (Grand Rapids, MI: Zondervan 2005); Hahn, "Kinship by Covenant," 592–593; Mark L. Strauss, *The Davidic Messiah in Luke-Acts: The Promise and Its Fulfillment in Lukan Christology* (New York: Continuum, 1995).

tells us in language drawn from the Old Testament purification rites (Heb. 1:3).[55] Through His priestly work, Christ "consecrated" believers (Heb. 2:10; 10:10), as previously God consecrated the Israelites (Ex. 31:13; Lev. 20:8; 21:15; Ezek. 20:12; 37:28). The Christian life is depicted as a living out of this priestly consecration. The believer, Hebrews says, has been consecrated and purified "in order to serve the living God" (Heb. 9:14; 12:28).

The "holy priesthood" of all the faithful is to render liturgical service, offering "spiritual sacrifices acceptable to God through Jesus Christ" (1 Pet. 2:5; Rom. 12:1).[56] Speaking in the sacrificial vocabulary of the Temple, Paul urges the Philippians to live as "without blemish" (Phil. 2:15) and exhorts them in the "sacrifice and liturgy of [their] faith." Life itself is here seen as liturgy (in Greek, *leitourgia*), with Paul adopting the Septuagint word for the ritual worship of God (*latreuein*) to define the Christian way of life.[57]

The highest expression of this liturgy of life is seen in believers' participation in the cosmic liturgy, the worship in heaven mediated by the high priest Christ. Hebrews describes the Eucharist as a "festal gathering" celebrated by the "church of the firstborn" with the angels on "Mount Zion ... the city of the living God, the heavenly Jerusalem."[58] The liturgy of the new covenant, the

---

[55] Compare Ex 29:37; 30:10; Lev 16:19; 2 Pet 1:9. Lane, *Hebrews 1–8*, 15.

[56] Raymond Corriveau, *The Liturgy of Life* (Brussels: Desclee De Brouwer, 1970).

[57] See, for example, Acts 24:14; 27:23; Rom 1:9; 2 Tim 1:3. See Corriveau, *The Liturgy of Life*, 141–142.

[58] Of course, many recent commentators reject the earliest interpreters of Hebrews and deny that there are Eucharistic references either here or elsewhere in the letter. I am persuaded otherwise. See Hahn, "Kinship by Covenant," 624–629.

Eucharist, forms the pattern of life for the firstborn of the new Family of God. Like the liberated Israelites, they no longer serve as slaves but as sons. By joining themselves sacramentally to the sacrifice of Christ, the sons and daughters were to offer themselves "through him" as a continual "sacrifice of praise" (Heb. 13:15).[59]

The Liturgical Consummation of the Canon

The New Testament also depicts the Church fulfilling the mission of Israel—to gather all nations to Zion to offer spiritual sacrifices of praise to God.[60] This is the vision we see in the Bible's last book. John's Apocalypse is a liturgical book. The literary evidence clearly indicates that the book was intended to be read in the liturgy, most likely in the celebration of the Eucharist "on the Lord's day," (Rev. 1:10).[61] The Apocalypse is also a book "about" liturgy. What is unveiled is nothing less than the liturgical consummation of human history in Christ. The vision John sees is that of a Eucharistic kingdom, in which angels and holy men and women worship ceaselessly around the altar and throne of God. The vision even unfolds in liturgical fashion, in a series of hymns, exhortations, antiphons, and other cultic forms.[62]

---

[59] William L. Lane, *Hebrews 9-13*, vol. 47b, *Word Biblical Commentary* (Nashville, TN: Thomas Nelson, 1991), 549, and William L. Lane, *Hebrews 1–8*.

[60] Wells, *God's Holy People*, 243.

[61] Ugo Vanni, "Liturgical Dialogue as a Literary Form in the Book of Revelation," *New Testament Studies* 37 (1991); David E. Aune, "The Apocalypse of John and the Problem of Genre," *Apocalypticism, Prophecy and Magic in Early Christianity* (Ada, MI: Baker Academic, 2008), 39–65.

[62] W. Hultitt Gloer, "Worship God! Liturgical Elements in the Apocalypse," *Review and Expositor* 98 (Winter 2001), 38–40.

Jesus, described throughout the book as "the Lamb," with obvious reference to the lamb of the Passover, brings about a new Exodus.[63] In this final book of the canon, we see the fulfillment of the canon's first book. In the new heaven and new earth, the new Jerusalem of Revelation, the children of the new Adam worship as priests and rule as kings, and the entire universe is revealed to have become a vast divine temple.[64]

Gathered together into this new paradise, those redeemed by the blood of the Lamb make up a priestly kingdom, as John sees it, quoting God's commission to Israel in Exodus 19:6 (Rev. 1:6; 5:10). But in this new kingdom, the children of Abraham reign with people from every tribe, tongue, and nation (Rev. 5:9; 7:9). Jesus is the "firstborn" of this new family of God, the prophesied root and offspring of David (Rev. 22:16; 3:7) in whom all are made divine sons and daughters of God (Rev. 21:7)—royal sons and priests who will rule with Him until the end of ages (Rev. 20:6).

Before the throne of God and the Lamb, the royal sons of God are shown worshipping Him, gazing upon His face with His name written upon their foreheads and reigning forever (Rev. 22:1–5). John chooses his words carefully here to evoke the Old Testament promises of God's intimate presence to those who serve Him. The word rendered "worship" in most translations of Rev. 22:3 is the Greek *latreusousin*—the word used in the Septuagint to translate

---

[63] Mathewson, *A New Heaven and a New Earth*, 62–64.
[64] William J. Dumbrell, *The End of the Beginning: Revelation 21–22 and the Old Testament* (Eugene, OR: Wipf & Stock, 2001).

the Hebrew word that describes Adam's original vocation as well as the purpose of the Exodus and conquest.[65]

At the conclusion of our liturgical reading of the canon, we hear the purpose and meaning of the entire Bible summed up in the refrain of the Apocalypse: "Worship God!" (Rev. 14:7; 19:10; 22:9). The human person has been shown from the first pages of Genesis to the last of Revelation to be liturgical by nature, created and destined to live in the spiritual house of creation, as children of a royal and priestly family that offers sacrifices of praise to their Father-Creator with whom they dwell in a covenant of peace and love.[66]

Towards a Liturgical Hermeneutic

Our liturgical reading of the canonical text reveals a clear liturgical *trajectory* and *teleology*. The story of the Bible is the story of humankind's journey to true worship in spirit and truth in the presence of God. That is the trajectory, the direction toward which narrative leads. This true worship is revealed to be the very purpose of God's creation in the beginning. That is the *teleology* revealed in the canonical text.

The formal unity of Scripture and liturgy and the recovery of the canonical text's liturgical teleology and trajectory has important methodological implications for biblical scholarship. Indeed, I would argue that three interpretive imperatives arise from our liturgical reading. These imperatives, which I will consider under the headings economy, typology, and mystagogy, undergird the assumptions of the

---

[65] Mathewson, *A New Heaven and a New Earth*, 205–206.
[66] Congar, *The Mystery of the Temple*, 192, 245–248.

biblical authors and present themselves as crucial dimensions that must be understood for any authentic interpretation of the text.

The Unity of Scripture: The Divine Economy

Our liturgical reading highlights the importance of what ancient Church writers called "the divine economy"—that is, the divine order of history as presented in the canonical text. Throughout the canonical narrative, the divine economy is presented as the motive for God's words and deeds.[67] The biblical writers understood the economy as part of "the mystery of his will, according to his purpose … a plan (*oikonomian*) for the fullness of time" (Eph. 1:9–10). In this the apostolic witness is faithful to the teaching of Christ, who is shown teaching them to see biblical history fulfilled in His life, death, and Resurrection (Lk. 24:26–27, 44–47).

As we have seen, the liturgy of both the old and new covenants is founded on remembrance and celebration of God's saving words and deeds. Liturgy, then, as presented in the Scripture, is an expression of faith in the divine economy and a means by which believers gain participation in that economy.[68] The Scriptures themselves are regarded

---

[67] For explanations of God's words and deeds in light of a divine covenant plan, see Ex 2:24; 6:5; 33:1; Num 32:11; Deut 1:8; 9:5; 30:20; 2 Sam 7:8, 10, 11, 22–25; 1 Chr 16:14–18; Jer 31:31–37; 33:14–26; Lk 1:46–55, 68–79; Acts 2:14–36; 3:12–26; 7:1–51; 11:34–43; 13:16–41.

[68] The purpose of Christian liturgy, says Dalmais, is "to express man's faith in the divine economy and perpetuate the living effects of the incarnation." Irénée Henri Dalmais, *Introduction to the Liturgy*, trans. Roger Capel (Baltimore: Helicon Press, 1961), 27. See also Jean Danielou, S. J., "The Sacraments and the History of Salvation," in *Liturgy and the Word of God* (Collegeville, MN: Liturgical Press, 1959), 29: "The object of faith is the existence of a divine plan."

by the biblical authors as the divinely inspired testament to the divine economy as it has unfolded throughout history, culminating in the saving event of the cross.

It follows that if our interpretations are to be true to the integrity of the texts, we must pay close attention to this notion of God's economy. The economy gives the Bible its content and unity.

The Typological Pattern

The divine economy is comprehended and explained in Scripture through a distinct way of reading and writing that originates in the canonical text and is carried over into the living Tradition of the faith community that gives us these texts. We characterize this way of reading and writing broadly as *typology*.[69]

In our liturgical reading, we observed the pervasiveness of typological patterns of exegesis in both the Old and New Testaments.[70] To recall but a few examples: The world's creation was portrayed in light of the later building of the tabernacle. The tabernacle in turn was described as a "new creation." Jesus' death and Resurrection are seen as a new passover and a new Exodus. The Christian sacramental life is illuminated by the Exodus event.

The extensive use of typology in the Scriptures reflects a profound biblical "worldview." If the economy gives narrative unity to the canonical Scriptures, fashioning

---

[69] See most recently, David Dawson, *Christian Figural Reading and the Fashioning of Identity* (Berkeley, CA: University of California Press, 2001); Christopher R. Seitz, *Figured Out: Typology and Providence in Christian Scripture* (Louisville, KY: Westminster John Knox Press, 2001).

[70] Michael Fishbane, *Biblical Interpretation in Ancient Israel* (Oxford, UK: Oxford University Press, 1989); Danielou, *The Bible and the Liturgy*, 5.

them into a single story, typology helps us to understand the full meaning of that story. Recognition of this biblical worldview has important hermeneutical implications. The interpreter of the Bible enters into a dialogue with a book that is itself an exegetical dialogue—a complex and highly cohesive interpretive web in which the meaning of earlier texts is discerned in the later texts and in which later texts can only be understood in relation to ones that came earlier.

In order to read the texts as they are written the exegete needs to acknowledge the authors' deep-seated belief in both the divine economy and in the typological expression of that economy. From our liturgical reading, we see that three moments in the economy of salvation stand out as having decisive typological significance for the entire canonical text—creation, the Exodus, and the Davidic kingdom. These in turn should have special significance for the exegete.

We must remain mindful that the foundation of all authentic biblical typology is the historical and literary sense of the text. Typology is not an arbitrary eisegesis. For the biblical authors, God uses historical events, persons, and places as material and temporal symbols or signs of future events and divine realities. The prophets can speak of a "new Exodus" only because they presuppose the historical importance of the original Exodus. The exegete likewise must see the literal and historical sense as fundamental to his or her approach to Scripture.

Mystagogy: Living the Scripture's Mysteries

The final hermeneutical imperative that emerges from our liturgical reading is *mystagogy*. Mystagogy recognizes that the same typological patterns by which the divine economy is comprehended in Scripture continue in the Church's sacramental liturgy. As we noted at the start of this paper, the canon was a liturgical enactment—the Scriptures come to us as the authoritative texts to be used in Christian teaching and worship. But, as it was written and passed on to us, Scripture has more than an instructional or exhortative function. When proclaimed in the Church's liturgy, Scripture is intended to "actualize" what is proclaimed—to bring the believer into living contact with the *mirabilia Dei*, the mighty saving works of God in the Old and New Testament.[71]

Mystagogy focuses our attention on the deep connection between the written "Word of God"—the Scripture itself—and the creative Word of God described in the pages of the Old and New Testaments. From the first pages to the last, we see expressed the biblical authors' faith that God's Word is living and active and possesses the power to bring into being what it commands. The Church's traditional understanding of the sacramental liturgy is built on this belief in the performative power of the Word of God as a "divine speech act."[72]

---

[71] "In principle, the liturgy, and especially the sacramental liturgy, the high point of which is the eucharistic celebration, brings about the most perfect actualization of the biblical texts, for the liturgy places the proclamation in the midst of the community of believers, gathered around Christ so as to draw near to God. ... Written *text thus becomes living word.*" Pontifical Biblical Commission, *Interpretation of the Bible in the Church* (March 18, 1994), IV, c, 1. Emphasis supplied.

[72] Timothy Ward, *Word and Supplement: Speech Acts, Biblical Texts, and the Sufficiency* (Oxford, UK: Oxford University Press, 2002); Kevin J. Vanhoozer, "From Speech Acts to Scripture Acts," in *After Pentecost: Language and Biblical Interpretation* (Grand Rapids, MI: Zondervan, 2001).

Proclaimed sacramentally and accompanied by the ritual washing of water, the Word brings the Spirit upon people making them sons and daughters of God through a real sharing in His life, death, and Resurrection (Rom. 6:3; Gal. 4:6; 1 Pet. 1:23). Proclaimed as commanded in the Eucharistic liturgy, the word brings about true participation in the one Body and Blood of Christ (1 Cor. 10:16–17). The Word in the sacramental liturgy continues the work of the Word in Scripture. This pattern, too, is shown originating in the pages of Scripture. The interpretation of Scripture is ordered to the celebration of Baptism (Acts 8:29–38) and the Eucharist (Lk. 24:27–31). The New Testament also gives us numerous passages in which the sacraments are explained "typologically," that is, according to events and figures in the Old Testament (1 Cor. 10; 1 Pet. 3:20–21). This paschal catechesis is at the heart of what early Church writers called *mystagogy*.[73]

At a minimum, then, our interpretations of Scripture must respect the mystagogic content of the New Testament. In this exegetes will do well to recall that the sacramental liturgy afforded the first interpretive framework for the Scriptures. But on a deeper level, the exegete must appreciate the *mystagogic intent* of the Bible. The exegete must always be conscious that the Word he or she interprets is written and preserved for the purpose of leading believers to the sacramental liturgy where they are brought into a covenant relationship with God.[74]

---

[73] Enrico Mazza, *Mystagogy: A Theology of Liturgy in the Patristic Age*, trans. M. J. O'Connell (Collegeville, MN: Liturgical Press, 1989).

[74] Danielou, "The Sacraments and the History of Salvation," 28, 31. See also J. A. DiNoia and Bernard Mulcahy, "The Authority of Scripture in Sacramental Theology," in *Pro Ecclesia*, 10 (2001), 329–45.

Towards a Liturgical Hermeneutic

I believe that, as a natural outgrowth of the past century's rediscovery of Scripture's liturgical sense, we are prepared for the development of a new, *liturgical hermeneutic*. As I have tried to sketch in this paper, this new hermeneutic is at once literary and historical, liturgical and sacramental. It will be capable of integrating the contributions of historical and literary research while at the same time respecting the traditional meanings given to the Bible by the believing community in which the Bible continues to serve as the source and wellspring of faith and worship. A liturgical hermeneutic will recognize the liturgical content and "mission" of the Bible—its mystagogic purpose in bringing about, through the sacramental liturgy, the communion of believers with the God who has chosen to reveal Himself in Scripture. It is, then, a hermeneutic that grasps the profound union of the divine Word incarnate in Christ, inspired in Scripture, and proclaimed in the Church's sacramental liturgy.

Much work remains to be done. But, I believe this understanding of Scripture has great potential to renew the study of the Bible from the heart of the Church. Reading Scripture liturgically, we will find no tension between letter and spirit, between the literary and historical analysis of Scripture and the faithful contemplation of its religious and spiritual meaning.

Life

And such is the force and power of the Word of God that it can serve the Church as her support and vigor, and the children of the Church as strength for their faith, food for the soul, and a pure and lasting fount of spiritual life.

— Dei Verbum, no. 21

The Cathedral: Where Heaven and Earth Meet

"Your bishop presides in the place of God."[1] So wrote St. Ignatius of Antioch, sometime around AD 107, as an escort of imperial soldiers transported the great bishop from his diocese in Syria to his execution in Rome.

I can remember reading that line in English and wondering about the phrase "the place of God." Did Ignatius mean "place" in the sense of *location*—meaning the *presence* or *company* of God? Or did he mean *place* in the sense of *vicarious representation*—meaning that the bishop is the agent of God's will?

My curiosity sent me back to the Greek text, where I learned that the answer is—both! It seems that the earliest documents disagree, due to an error in transcription. Where we read "place," some ancient manuscripts use the Greek word *topos* (location) while others say *typos* (representative).[2] We will almost certainly never know which word St. Ignatius originally used, so we are left with a providential "typo," a happy fault of some anonymous copyist.

This essay first appeared as "The Cathedral: Where Heaven and Earth Meet," in *A Reflection of Faith: St. Paul Cathedral, Pittsburgh 1906–2006* (Pittsburgh: St. Paul Cathedral, 2007), 13–18.

[1] Ignatius, *Letter to the Magnesians*, no. 6. Unless otherwise noted, translations are composite or original.

[2] *The Epistles of St. Clement of Rome and St. Ignatius of Antioch*, vol. 1 of *Ancient Christian Writers*, tr. James A. Kleist, S. J. (New York: Newman Press, 1946), 128, no. 19.

I say this because both senses of *place* are true, and the two are inseparable. The bishop presides as God's vicar in a particular diocese. And the bishop presides in God's house—His holy temple—which is the cathedral. It would be impossible to speak of the cathedral as God's house without speaking of the bishop as the image of God's fatherhood on earth.

Our word cathedral has a rich scriptural pedigree. It comes from *kathedra*, which means "seat of honor" and appears in the Septuagint and other Greek versions of the Old Testament. Jesus uses the word in this sense in only one place, but His choice is significant: "The scribes and the Pharisees sit on Moses' seat (*kathedra Mouseos*); so practice and observe whatever they tell you" (Mt. 23:2–3). *Kathedra* here is a seat of religious and moral authority, from which wise men teach and guide. The German scholar Alexander Sand has written that "the *kathedra Mouseos* belonged as a seat of honor to the permanent furniture of the synagogue. . . . It was the official teaching chair for the scribes and Pharisees. . . . Their teaching is binding upon the people."[3] Jesus, indeed, distinguishes this "teaching chair" from other seats that were merely honorific; for these latter He used a different, though related Greek word (see Mt. 23:6, *protokathedriai*).

In the wider Greek-speaking world, *kathedra* represented the chair from which philosophers taught their pupils. Thus, whether Jew or Greek, the man who occupied the *kathedra* was acknowledged to be the teacher and guide of the community.

---

[3] Alexander Sand, "Kathedra," in *Exegetical Dictionary of the New Testament*, vol. 2 (Grand Rapids MI: Eerdmans Publishing, 1991), 221.

In establishing the new covenant, Jesus did not abolish the old or its covenant structures. He assumed to Himself the roles of Israel's teachers and priests, prophets and king, and these He delegated to His apostles. Though the *kathedra* was superior to other seats of honor, He assigned to the Twelve something still greater. "Jesus said to them, 'Truly, I say to you, in the new world, when the Son of man shall sit on his glorious throne, you who have followed me will also sit on twelve thrones, judging the twelve tribes of Israel'" (Mt. 19:28). He promised them thrones (*thronoi*), that is, judgment seats suitable for kings.

The apostles would occupy these exalted thrones but they called their position by a rather workaday name: *episkope*, which the old English translations rendered as "bishopric," though it literally means "office" (see Acts 1:20). The office-holder was called simply "the office-holder" or "overseer"—in Greek, *episkopos*, from which we get the word "episcopacy." These men—like Timothy, for example (see 1 Tim. 3:1)—received their office, their succession, from the hands of the apostles themselves. They, in turn, each in his own city, would occupy the *kathedra* that was greater than the seat of Moses. They would, as St. Ignatius said, "preside in the place of God."

Archeological digs have unearthed early Christian house churches side by side with Jewish synagogues. They resemble one another in design and decoration.[4] Certainly

---

[4] On the excavations at Dura Europos, see Jack Finegan, *Light from the Ancient Past* (Princeton, N.J.: Princeton University, 1946), 403ff. On the nearness of Christian and Jewish houses of worship, see Rodney Stark, *The Rise of Christianity* (San Francisco: HarperCollins, 1997), 68–69. On the raised seats in both synagogues and churches, see Steven J. Schloeder, *Architecture in Communion* (San Francisco: Ignatius, 1998), 86ff.; also Louis Bouyer, *Liturgy*

the first Christians kept the *kathedra* as a permanent furnishing in their places of worship. This seat was occupied by the bishop, whose throne represented his authority to teach, rule, and sanctify. Throughout the era of the Church Fathers—and fairly consistently throughout the Christian world—the bishop preached not from a pulpit, but from his *kathedra*, where he remained seated. Latinized as *cathedra*, the word would come to stand for the bishop's office, his authority, and indeed his church, the *cathedral*, the place where he habitually conducted his teaching, preaching, and liturgical blessing.

The Church's understanding of the bishop's office was well established at a very early date. Keep in mind that Ignatius's lifetime overlapped with the lives of the apostles. He was either the second or third successor to St. Peter as bishop of Antioch; and some traditions hold that he was tutored by St. John the Apostle. With the apostles so near, Ignatius felt compelled to keep and defend the dignity of his apostolic office: "We should regard the bishop as we would the Lord himself,"[5] he told the Christians of Ephesus. If the bishop stood in the place of the Lord, then Christians should stand with him: "For all those who belong to God and to Jesus Christ are also with the bishop."[6]

The people stood by their bishop, most often, in his Church, before his *kathedra*. In Ignatius's day, the bishop was the ordinary minister of the sacraments. The priests (*presbyteroi*) and deacons (*diakonoi*) were prominent in the

and Architecture (Notre Dame: Notre Dame University Press, 1967), 10–11, 25–26, 32–34, 43–45.

[5] St. Ignatius, *Letter to the Ephesians*, no. 6.
[6] St. Ignatius, *Letter to the Philadelphians*, no. 3.

life of the Antiochene Church as they were in the New Testament Church of the apostles. But if the priests and deacons presided at the sacraments, they did so only as the bishop's delegates.

> Let no man do anything connected with the Church without the bishop. Let that be deemed a proper Eucharist which is administered either by the bishop or by one to whom he has entrusted it. Wherever the bishop shall appear, there let the assembly also be—just as, wherever Jesus Christ is, there is the Catholic Church. It is not lawful to baptize or to hold a love-feast without the consent of the bishop. On the other hand, whatever has his approval is pleasing to God.[7]

It was customary for the bishop to celebrate the local Church's liturgy assisted by his entire clergy, and surrounded by the assembly of the baptized believers of his city. Ignatius spoke of this as "a divine harmony"[8] as he described the tripartite structure of the clergy: "Your bishop presides in the place of God, and your presbyters in the place of the assembly of the apostles, along with your deacons." It is "divine" because it mirrors something revealed of heaven. Commentators have long noted the similarity between Ignatius's description and the scene that John the Seer envisioned in the Book of Revelation. There, twenty-four elders (*presbyteroi*, or priests) stand in a semicircle about the throne of God, where they are joined by many worshipping creatures who sing "Holy, holy, holy is

---

[7] St. Ignatius, *Letter to the Smyrnaeans*, no. 8.
[8] Ibid., no. 8.

the Lord God Almighty."[9] Thus, as God presided over the liturgy in heaven, surrounded by His apostles and saints, so the bishop presided "in God's place" over the liturgy on earth, surrounded by his clergy and congregation.

Yet there was, for both Ignatius and John, not two liturgies, but one. This is an important doctrine and something that distinguished early Christianity from Judaism of the Second Temple period and earlier Israelite religion. The people of ancient Israel considered their earthly liturgy to be a divinely inspired imitation of heavenly worship. Both Moses and Solomon constructed God's earthly dwellings—the tabernacle and the Temple—according to a heavenly archetype revealed by God Himself (see Ex. 25:8–9; 1 Chron. 28:19; Wis. 9:8,). The prophets expressed this belief in a mystical way, as they depicted the angels worshiping amid songs and trappings that were clearly recognizable from the Jerusalem Temple (see Is. 6:1–7). The hymns sung by the angels were the same songs the Levites sang before the earthly sanctuary. What the priests did in the Temple sanctuary was an earthly imitation of what the angels did in heaven.

Yet it was still only a shadow of the angel's worship—and only a shadow of the earthly worship that would be inaugurated in the age of the Messiah.

---

[9] Revelation 4; cf. Dom Gregory Dix, *The Shape of the Liturgy* (New York: Seabury, 1982), 28f. See also the *Didascalia Apostolorum* (third or fourth century A.D.): "And for the priests let there be separated a place on the eastern side of the house, and let the bishop's chair be among them." *The Didascalia Apostolorum in Syriac*, ed. and trans., A. Voobus (Louvain: CSCO, 1979), nos. 130–131. I treat this subject at length in my book *The Lamb's Supper* (New York: Doubleday, 1999).

By assuming human flesh, the eternal Son of God brought heaven to earth. No longer must the People of God worship in imitation of angels. In the liturgy of the new covenant, Christ Himself presides, and we not only imitate the angels; we participate with them.

This is what Ignatius saw from the *kathedra* in his Antiochene Church, and what he described in his *Letter to the Magnesians*. And this, moreover, is what bishops today accomplish as they preside "in the place of God" at the liturgy of heaven and earth. The archbishop of Vienna, Cardinal Christoph Schonborn, wrote recently: "in the Eucharist heaven already comes down to earth, and the earthly church opens herself upward to her heavenly home."[10]

After the Exodus from Egypt, as Israel sojourned in the desert, God gave Moses "the pattern of the tabernacle, and of all its furniture" (Ex. 25:9). And so Moses commanded the construction of this portable sanctuary of God's presence among His chosen people. Centuries later, in Jerusalem, God gave David "the plan of the vestibule of the Temple, and of its houses, its treasuries, its upper rooms, and its inner chambers, and of the room for the mercy seat" (1 Chron. 28:11). To the son of David, King Solomon, God also gave the right to call His Temple "the house of the LORD" and "the house of God" (1 Chron. 28:20–21).

The early Christians saw both the tabernacle and the Temple as biblical "types" foreshadowing the Christian Church. They were earthly sanctuaries that would find

---

[10] Christoph von Schönborn, *Living the Catechism of the Catholic Church*, vol. 2: *The Sacraments*, trans. John Saward (San Francisco: Ignatius, 2000), 100.

their fulfillment in the worship of heaven and earth that we find detailed in the New Testament books of Hebrews and Revelation (Heb. 8–10; Rev. 11:19). The Church at worship included what Catholics traditionally call the Church Militant, the Church Triumphant, and the Church Suffering—the great cloud of witnesses—the communion of the Church on earth, in heaven, and in purgatory.

When the early Christians spoke of the Church this way, they meant, of course, the Universal Church considered in its entirety, but they also meant the particular Church, the local community, and even each Church building. For each altar was, for them, the place where heaven touched down to earth in the Eucharist. Today, in some of the Oriental Christian Churches—which have preserved much of the primitive Christian vocabulary—churches are still called "temples." (Indeed, tourists will find this terminology as they read the inscriptions on the older churches in Rome.) For the early Christians, the bishop "presided in the place of God"—that is, in His earthly house, His earthly temple, which is now united in worship with the heavenly sanctuary.

In the ancient *Didascalia Apostolorum* ("The Teaching of the Apostles"), at least as old as the third or fourth century, posterity has left us a profound biblical theology of the bishop's role in God's Church.

> Today, then, you too, O bishops, are priests to your people, and Levites who minister to the tabernacle of God, the holy Catholic Church, who stand continually before the Lord God. You, then, are to your people priests and prophets, and princes and leaders and kings, and mediators between God and his faithful, and receivers of the word, and its preachers and proclaimers. You are

knowers of the Scriptures and of the utterances of God, and witnesses of his will, who bear the sins of all, and are to give an answer for all. . . . As you have taken up the burden of all, so the fruits also which you receive from all the people shall be yours, for all things of which you have need. Nourish well those who are in want, as if to render an account to him who will require it, who can make no mistake nor be evaded. For as you administer the office of the bishopric, so from the same office of the bishopric ought you to be nourished, as the priests and Levites and ministers who serve before God, as it is written in the Book of Numbers.[11]

The bishops are to guide, provide, teach, nourish, mediate, receive honor and respect, and take responsibility for their congregation. In short, they are to play the same role a father plays in a domestic family. This, too, is an idea with deep Old Testament roots. In the patriarchal period—the time of Noah, Abraham, and Jacob—there was no priestly class or order. In each family, the father functioned as a priest, a leader in prayer and sacrifice, a teacher, and intercessor. This remained the sacred family order through the periods of slavery in Egypt and wandering in the desert. The fathers of Israel lost this privilege only when they sinned grievously by worshipping the golden calf. Only the tribe of Levi remained faithful to God, and so only they retained their priesthood. Yet, even then, the priestly function remained a fatherly one. In the Book of Judges, we read that, when a Levite appeared at the door of Micah, Micah pleaded, "Stay with me, and be to me a father and

---

[11] *Didascalia Apostolorum*, no. 8.

a priest" (Judg. 17:10). A chapter later, Micah's plea was echoed, almost verbatim, by the Danites as they invited the Levite to be priest for their entire tribe: "Come with us, and be to us a father and a priest" (Judg. 18:19). That call echoed still in the hearts of the first Christians.

Presiding in the place of God, a bishop cannot be anything but a father, because "Father" is *who God is* and *what God does*. Ignatius knew this and so he dared to compare himself with God the Father. The apostle Paul had done no less: "For this reason I bend my knees to the Father, from whom all fatherhood in heaven and on earth receives its name" (Eph. 3:14–15). (The Greek word sometimes translated "fatherhood" and sometimes "family" is *patria*, in Latin, *paternitas*, from which we get the English *paternity*.)

In his brilliant analysis of Ignatius's letters, the British scholar Gregory Dix wrote: "If the bishop had a special representative function it must therefore be as the 'father of the family' of God. . . . It was, in our still surviving phrase as 'father in God' that the bishop sat enthroned as 'the image of God' and the 'type of the Father.'"[12]

Dix points out that, in the ancient church, the bishop exercised his teaching function sitting at his *kathedra*, his throne, but his priestly function standing at the altar. Yet both are fatherly functions, and the liturgy itself culminates in a supremely divine fatherly action, fulfilled by the bishop. The oldest surviving rubric for Holy Communion is the following, from the *Apostolic Tradition* of St. Hippolytus (ca. AD 215): "And when the bishop breaks

---

[12] Dix, *The Shape of the Liturgy*, 30.

the bread, in distributing to each a fragment he shall say: 'The Bread of Heaven in Christ Jesus.'"[13] In this, as in all things, the bishop presides in the place of God. His distribution of Communion is an earthly image of the Father's sending of the Son. As Jesus told the congregation at the synagogue of Capernaum: "My Father gives you the true bread from heaven" (Jn. 6:32).

And what of the *cathedra*, the bishop's chair that embodies his office? Dix concludes: "The throne of the bishop was in reality—as the Apocalypse expressed it—'the throne of God and the Lamb'" (Rev. 22:3).

Here, at the *cathedra*, is the "place of God," and here is where the bishop presides—in God's place, as God's typic image. In the cathedral liturgy—today as in the time of the apostles—heaven comes to earth. That is an astonishing fact. And we find it proclaimed by the Church in the farewell letters of Ignatius of Antioch as in the 1993 *Catechism of the Catholic Church*. In the latter we read: "The liturgy is the work of the whole Christ, head and body. Our high priest celebrates it unceasingly in the heavenly liturgy, with the holy Mother of God, the apostles, all the saints, and the multitude of those who have already entered the kingdom" (Catechism, no. 1187). "Those who even now celebrate it without signs are already in the heavenly liturgy, where celebration is wholly communion and feast" (Catechism, no. 1136).[14]

I was flush with the pride of discovery.

---

[13] St. Hippolytus, *Apostolic Tradition*, no. 23.5, quoted in Dix, *The Shape of the Liturgy*, 30.
[14] See also CCC, nos. 1090, 1111, 1326.

Chapter Six

Matthew: Gospel of Fulfillment

The paper I'd just presented to a doctoral seminar on the Gospel of Matthew was important and original. I was convinced of it. Even the grueling, two-and-a-half-hour session of questioning by my professor and fellow students had left me—and my thesis—unscathed.

I argued that Matthew's account of Jesus giving Peter the "keys to the kingdom" cites an obscure oracle of Isaiah about the transfer of "the key of the House of David." What Jesus confers upon Peter—namely, authority over His Church—corresponds to what Isaiah's king confers upon Eliakim in making him prime minister of the Davidic kingdom.

Earlier scholars, both Protestant and Catholic, had noticed the Isaiah citation. And you don't have to be a scholar to notice that Matthew is filled with quotations, citations, allusions and echoes from the Old Testament.

I felt I had a fresh insight, however, in seeing how the citation helps us understand Matthew's meaning and Jesus' intention. As I saw it, the passage depicts Jesus as the new Davidic king and the Church as the restored kingdom of David.

A Catholic "Key"

It was this conclusion and others like it that eventually led me to become a Catholic.

It wasn't long after I entered the Church that I encountered these biblical passages again—in a setting I was hardly expecting.

It happened one day at Mass. The first reading was taken from Isaiah 22, the same obscure oracle I'd studied in such detail for my paper. Now, that's an interesting coincidence, I thought. A few minutes later, the priest proclaimed the Gospel: Matthew 16—Jesus giving the keys to Peter!

What were the odds of those two Scriptures being read at the same Mass? I asked myself. At the time, I was learning a lot of things about being a Catholic, including how the Church's liturgy worked. I felt as if I'd hit some kind of lectionary lottery.

Only later did I discover that the readings we hear at Mass aren't chosen by holy happenstance. My innovative interpretation of Matthew 16 was one that Catholics had been hearing in the liturgy for years.

The Biblical "Type"

In the nearly 20 years since I became a Catholic, I've had this experience again and again in the liturgy.

Sunday after Sunday, the Church gives us a pattern of biblical interpretation, showing us how the promises of the Old Testament are fulfilled in the New Testament. It's no wonder the Church does it this way. The Church learned this from the New Testament writers, who learned it from Jesus.

The evangelists understood the Old Testament as salvation history, the patient unfolding of God's gracious and merciful plan to fashion the human race into a family of God that worships and dwells with Him.

Some early believers wanted to throw out the Old Testament as irrelevant. But those people were quickly branded as heretics. For the early Church, Israel's story was their family story.

The words and deeds, historical figures and events in the Old Testament concealed deeper layers of meaning, meanings only fully revealed with the coming of Jesus. The flood and Noah's ark were "types" or signs to prepare us to understand the saving work of baptism and the Church. The manna God gave the Israelites in the desert was also a "type" of the true bread from heaven that God would give us in the Eucharist.

The *Catechism of the Catholic Church* calls this way of reading "typology" (see nos. 128–130; 1094–1095). Typology is the guiding principle the Church uses in selecting the readings we hear at Mass. As the Pontifical Biblical Commission said in its important 1993 document, *The Interpretation of the Bible in the Church*: "By regularly associating a text of the Old Testament with the text of the Gospel, the cycle often suggests a scriptural interpretation moving in the direction of typology" (IV. c. 1).

The New Hidden in the Old

All this is important to keep in mind as we read Matthew's Gospel Sunday by Sunday over the course of the liturgical year (as we do in "Cycle A" of the lectionary readings).

With Matthew, we have a master of typology. Matthew's Gospel is a prime example of what St. Augustine was talking about when he said that the New Testament is concealed in the Old and the Old Testament is revealed in the New.

You can't read Matthew without having your ear tuned to the Old Testament, from which he quotes or to which he alludes four or five times per chapter, more than 100 times in his Gospel.

Matthew writes this way because he wants his fellow Israelites to see that their covenant with God has been fulfilled in Jesus. Get used to words like "fulfill" and "fulfillment"! You're going to find them repeatedly in Matthew's Gospel.

On the Fourth Sunday of Advent, for instance, Matthew explains how Mary is found with child: "All this took place to fulfill what the Lord had spoken by the prophet: 'Behold, a virgin shall conceive and bear a son, and his name shall be called Emmanuel'" (Mt. 1:22–23). (All citations in this chapter are from Matthew, unless otherwise noted.)

Again, on Palm Sunday, when Jesus is arrested in the garden, He says: "But all this has taken place, that the scriptures of the prophets might be fulfilled" (26:56).

The Promised Son

The numerous fulfillments Matthew tells us about are intended to signal one thing: in Jesus, God is finally delivering on the promises He made throughout salvation history.

Matthew announces this in his very first line, which we hear in the Christmas Vigil Mass: "The book of the genealogy of Jesus Christ, the son of David, the son of Abraham" (1:1).

In this one sentence, Matthew drops four critical Old Testament references and he expects his readers—including you and me—to get them.

First, the word we translate as "genealogy" is *genesis*, the Greek word for "creation" and, of course, the name of the Bible's first book. Matthew also evokes God's covenants with Abraham and David, both of which involved a promise of divinely given sons.

At the dawn of salvation history, God made His covenant with Abraham, promising him an heir whose descendants would be as countless as the stars in the sky, a chosen people through whom God would bestow His blessings on all the earth (see Gen. 22:16–18). Centuries later, when the descendants of Abraham had become a mighty kingdom, God made a climactic covenant with David, His hand-picked and anointed king.

By an "eternal covenant," God promised that David's son would be His own son and that He would reign forever, not only over Israel, but also over all the nations. (To read more about the Davidic covenant, see 2 Sam. 7:8–16; 23:5; Ps. 2:7–8 and 72:8, 11.) In effect, God's covenant with David is a promise to finally fulfill His covenant with Abraham—making Abraham's descendants, gathered into the kingdom ruled by David's son, the everlasting source of blessings for all the world.

Unfortunately, David's kingdom crumbled, and the people were swept away into exile about four hundred years after David died. This "Babylonian exile" is the turning point in Matthew's genealogy. He repeats the phrase four times so we don't miss it (1:11 and 12, and twice in verse 17).

This is his way of showing us that Jesus is the Christ (*Messiah* in Hebrew) the prophets had hoped for, the new son of David who would liberate Israel from its enemies, restore the lost sheep to the house of Israel, and establish a new covenant that would embrace all nations. (For background on some of these prophecies, see Is. 2:2–3; 7:14; 9:1–7; 11:1–5, 10; 42:6; 55:3–5; Jer. 23:5–6; 31:31–34; 32:36–41; Ezek. 16:59–63; 34:24–30; 37:23–28.)

In that first sentence, Matthew gives us a summary of his Gospel and the entire New Testament. It is a book about the new world created by Jesus, the Christ sent to fulfill God's ancient covenant promises to David and Abraham.

New Moses, New Exodus

In showing us how Jesus fulfills God's promises, Matthew wants us to see the connections between His life and that of the first great deliverer of Israel, Moses.

Especially in his early chapters, Matthew wants you to hear lots of familiar echoes: What figure before Jesus is born under threat of death, facing a tyrannical ruler who has decreed that all firstborn Hebrew males are to be killed? What other figure in salvation history is saved by family members and remains in exile until those seeking his life are dead? (To compare the stories, read Mt. 2:13–20 and Ex. 1:15–16; 2:1–10; 4:19.) Not once in all this does Matthew say, "Jesus' early life looks a lot like Moses.'" He doesn't have to.

This understanding of Jesus as a "new Moses" continues throughout Matthew's Gospel.

As Israel passed through the waters of the Red Sea, so God's beloved son, Jesus, too passes through water in His baptism and is also called God's Son. (cf. Mt. 3:17 with Ex. 4:22.) As Israel left the waters to be tested in the desert for forty years, following His baptism Jesus was immediately driven into the wilderness to be tested for forty days and forty nights.

When you hear the story of Jesus' testing by the devil on the First Sunday of Lent, be sure to notice how His temptations correspond to Israel's in the wilderness (see Mt. 4:1–11).

First, Jesus is tempted by hunger, which had caused Israel to grumble against God. Then He is dared to put God to the test, to question God's care for Him. This recalls the Israelites' testing of God at Meribah and Massah. Finally, He is tempted to worship a false god, which Israel actually did in creating the golden calf. (To read about Israel's temptations, see Ex. 16:1–13; 17:1–6; 32:1–35.)

Notice also that each time Jesus rebukes the devil, He quotes Moses. Each quote is carefully chosen from a key section in the Book of Deuteronomy in which Moses warns the people to learn a lesson from their unfaithfulness in the desert. (Compare Jesus' words to Deut. 6:12–16; 8:3.)

As Moses climbed a mountain to bring the people the Law of God and the covenant, Jesus climbs a "mount" and delivers a new Law and a new covenant. Moses commanded the Israelites to commemorate God's covenant in the Passover celebration (see Ex. 12). Jesus institutes a new Passover, the Eucharist. As Moses sealed the old covenant with the blood of sacrificial animals, Jesus seals the new covenant with His own blood, and even quotes Moses' words: "This is the blood of my covenant." (cf. Mt. 26:28 and Ex. 24:8.)

Matthew sees Jesus leading a new Exodus: this time, not from a political tyrant whose armies are drowned in the sea, but from sin and death, which are destroyed in the waters of baptism.

It can't be stressed enough that, for Matthew, this is salvation history, not literary allusion. Matthew isn't writing a clever story designed to evoke memories of Moses and the Exodus. Matthew, like all devout Jews of the time, believed that God's saving words and deeds in the past formed a kind of template for what God would say and do to save Israel in the future.

Moses himself had promised that a prophet like him would one day arise (see Deut. 18:15). And the prophets increasingly talked about a "new Exodus" that would return the scattered Israelites and bring them to Zion for a great festal gathering with all the nations (see Is. 10:25–27; 11:15–16; 43:2, 16–19; 51:9–11; Jer. 23:7–8; 31:31–33).

Matthew sees Jesus doing the same things that Mark and Luke saw Him doing. But in writing his account, he wants us to see how in doing these things, Jesus is fulfilling God's promises.

David's Kingdom Comes (Again)

As Jesus moves closer to Jerusalem, Matthew shows us a different Old Testament pattern emerging in the life of Jesus. Actually, from the very start, he has told us that he believes Jesus to be the new Son of David and restorer of the Davidic kingdom.

On the Third Sunday in Ordinary Time, Jesus announces "the kingdom" for the first time. Matthew adds a curious detail—that Jesus is in Galilee, in the region of Zebulun and Naphtali (4:13). Why do we need to know that? Because that's where David's kingdom started to crumble, when Assyria invaded this very region some seven hundred years earlier (see 2 Kings 15:29).

Isaiah predicted God would begin restoring the fallen kingdom precisely where its disintegration began. And Matthew sees Jesus fulfilling this prophecy (see Mt. 4:12–17 and Is. 9:1–2, 7). That's why, when we hear this Gospel on the Third Sunday in Ordinary Time, we'll also hear the reading from Isaiah.

The Kingdom's Keys

Perhaps the pivot of the Gospel is Matthew 16—the scene that kept me up nights as a doctoral student—the giving of "the keys" to Peter. As Catholics, we've all heard the story. But we need to listen to it again in a "Davidic key."

Simon's confession that Jesus is "the Christ, the Son of the Living God" brings together the most important titles the prophets and psalmists had used to describe the promised son of David. He was to be the "anointed one" ("the Christ") and "the Son of God" (see Ps. 2:2, 7; 89:27; 2 Sam. 7:14).

Jesus changes Simon's name to Peter (Greek for "rock"), and tells him: "On this rock I will build my church" (16:18).

In His Sermon on the Mount, Jesus had spoken of "a wise man who built his house on rock" (7:24). This was a subtle reference to Solomon, who was revered for his wisdom (see 1 Kings 3:10–12) and who built the Temple on a rock (see 1 Kings 5:17; 7:10). Matthew sees Jesus as the new Solomon, the new Son of David, building a new spiritual temple—His Church—on the "rock" of Peter's faith.

As Isaiah had foretold, the keys of David's kingdom would be given to a new royal steward or prime minister. Isaiah promised that this prime minister would be a father over Jerusalem and would have full authority: what "he opens, no one shall shut." So Jesus gives Peter the keys and the power to "bind" and "loose" (Mt. 16:19; for Isaiah's prophecy, see Is. 22:20–24).

A King's Reception

When Jesus finally reaches Jerusalem, Matthew paints us a picture that looks a lot like the Old Testament scene of the anointing and crowning of David's son Solomon. (cf. Mt. 21:1–11 and 1 Kings 1:38–45.) In case we don't get the subtle allusions he makes, Matthew depicts the crowd crying out to Jesus as the "Son of David."

And the drama in Matthew's final pages turns on whether Jesus is in fact the Davidic Messiah. Note how often the Davidic phrases—"Son of David," "Son of God," and "King of the Jews"—appear in these pages.

Matthew leaves no doubt where he stands. In the last scene of his Gospel, he depicts Jesus as the king's heir. As God had promised to David, Jesus is the Son of God, given "all power" over "all nations" until the "end of the age" (28:18–20).

Matthew's Gospel of fulfillment is complete: Jesus is the long-awaited Son of David and Son of God. His Church is the restored Kingdom of David, which will be the font of blessing for all nations—fulfilling the covenant that God made with Abraham at the dawn of salvation history.

Written Text, Living Word

With Jesus' parting words, "I am with you always" (Mt. 28:20)," Matthew points us back to the first of His Old Testament fulfillments—that the Messiah's name would be Emmanuel or "God is with us."

The divine mission has been accomplished, He is telling us. God's plan for history has been realized. Jesus has taught us to pray to God as our Father and has given us the means of becoming beloved sons and daughters in baptism. And in the Eucharist and the Church, He is with us always.

This is what God desired from the first pages of the Old Testament, when He walked with Adam and Eve in the cool of the day—to dwell with His people that all might share in the divine presence.

We hear God's desire in one of the most beautiful Davidic prophecies: Ezekiel's promise of a new King David to rule the nations by an "everlasting covenant" in which God would dwell with His people forever (see Ezek. 37:24–28).

This is the promise Matthew sees fulfilled in the Paschal Mystery of Christ. But this divine fulfillment is not one of termination but of continuation.

Salvation history continues in the liturgy, which we celebrate at Christ's command. In this sacred memorial, the sacred words of Scripture perform a sacred deed—changing bread and wine into His Body and Blood. "Written text thus becomes living Word," as the Pontifical Biblical

Commission has said so well. By this living Word proclaimed in the liturgy, your life story and mine are joined to the story of salvation begun in the Scriptures.

I learned this by surprise as a new Catholic. You can relive my "discovery" on the 21st Sunday in Ordinary Time when the Liturgy of the Word again pairs the reading of Isaiah 22 with Matthew 16. But we can all share in this dynamic experience every Sunday, as we hear the Old Testament revealed in the New, as the written text is once more made living Word.

Chapter Seven

The Times of the Signs:
Toward a Biblical Approach to "Pentecostal" Phenomena

Many people believe we are living amid a new outpouring of the Holy Spirit. In 1960, Pope John XXIII, when asked why he was convening the Second Vatican Council, replied that he was praying for a "new Pentecost."

No one knows how literally he meant it. But some Catholics believe God took His vicar at his word, and poured out His Spirit in astonishing new ways. First, there was the teaching of the Council itself—vital, timely, and profound in its pastoral implications. Then, in the decades that followed, we saw remarkable signs of the Spirit's work: ordinary men and women empowered to teach and heal, who have also seemingly manifested charismatic gifts not seen since the first century (e.g., speaking in tongues).

Some people responded by saying such phenomena were altogether valid—and should even be normative for Catholics—while others rejected all of it as fraudulent. If we *don't* reject it all as pure fraud, we're left with the question: What does it mean?

But, before we can read the pentecostal signs of our times, we need to deepen our understanding of Pentecost itself in the light of Scripture.

Pentecosts, New and Old

Even schoolchildren should know that the feast of Pentecost was a New Testament event. Just fifty days after Easter, ten days after Jesus ascended into heaven, the Holy Spirit descended upon the apostles in power, causing them to speak in tongues and prophesy.

Yet few Christians know that even that day had its precedents—that God had sent His Spirit in similar ways, amid similar circumstances, back in Old Testament times, and with strikingly similar results. Both Pentecosts, old and new, can help us understand our own times of the Spirit.

Pentecost was first an *Israelite* festival—celebrated fifty days after Passover—commemorating the lawgiving at Mount Sinai. But something more than stone tablets was given to Moses in the Sinai wilderness.

Moses needed help to bear the burden of leadership, so God "took some of the spirit that was upon him and put it upon the seventy elders" (Num. 11:25). Empowered by God, these elders began to prophesy. Moses proclaimed his wish that "all the LORD's people were prophets, that the LORD would put his spirit upon them" (Num. 11:29).

With such special graces, you'd think that Israel would have begun an era of peace and faithfulness. But instead they rebelled, instigating a series of revolts against authorities, at every level. The people, the priests, the elders—even Aaron himself—rebelled. Though this new era began with great blessings, it soon degenerated into immorality, idolatry, and dissent. The ordinary faithful found it difficult to adjust to this new situation—whom should they follow? How should they know whom to trust? Thus they wandered for forty years, till the last of the unbelievers had perished in the desert.

What good did the outpouring of the Spirit do?

Judging from appearances, you might say it did nothing but trigger confusion. However, upon closer analysis, we'll see that the blessings were not the cause of the confusion, but rather provisions to help the faithful through it all. God had foreseen the confusion that would come with rebellion. He poured out His Spirit on Moses and the seventy, so that the people who really wanted to hear God's Word would hear it.

The First Joel

Now let's move from the old covenant Pentecost to the New. Fifty days after Jesus' death and Resurrection at Passover, the apostles were gathered in Jerusalem to celebrate Pentecost. On that occasion, God poured out His spirit—in a powerful, new way—upon all of the hundred and twenty gathered in the Upper Room. As a result, they all began to prophesy and speak in tongues, from the greatest to the least. When pressed for an explanation, Peter quoted the prophet Joel: "And in the last days it shall be, God declares, that I will pour out my Spirit upon all flesh, and your sons and your daughters shall prophesy … yea, and on my menservants and my maidservants in those days I will pour out my Spirit; and they shall prophesy" (Acts 2:17–18; Joel 2:28–32).

Don't miss the significance of this. Moses' wish for Israel was now coming true. Not just the elders would prophesy, but the sons and daughters—and even the hired help.

Also, not to be missed is the significance of Joel's original prophecy, from which Peter quotes. In the very next line, Joel delivers an ominous warning: "For in Jerusalem there shall be those who escape" (Joel 2:32).

Joel had good news and bad news for Jerusalem. The good news is that God's Spirit is preparing a faithful remnant to see their way through a time of great trials and confusion. The bad news is that most would be lost.

When Peter quoted Joel, he must have noticed the larger context. After all, what was Jesus' last prediction, right before His arrest? In Jerusalem, "there will not be left here one stone upon another, that will not be thrown down. . . . This generation will not pass away till all these things take place" (Mt. 24:2, 34).

He uttered those words between AD 30 and 33. A generation in Jesus' time was forty years. Within forty years, Roman legions laid waste to Jerusalem. All told, 1.1 million Jews perished in that siege.

Peter saw it clearly. The Messiah had come, and Israel had rebelled—just as they did in Moses' time—beginning with the High Priest who ordered Jesus' execution. Then the rebellion spread, from the scribes and priests to the Pharisees and Sadducees, until the ordinary faithful were hopelessly confused.

Given such chaos, how would the Father provide for the needs of His children?

By now, all of this should begin to sound familiar. In Moses' day, God had sent His Spirit at the beginning of forty years of chaos. Likewise, in Peter's day, forty years before judgment befell Jerusalem, the Spirit came down, and men and women began to prophesy and speak in tongues.

Utter Mysteries

But it's reasonable for us to ask: what is God's purpose for tongue-speaking?

First, let's consider St. Paul's take on the matter: "One who speaks in a tongue speaks not to men but to God; for no one understands him, but he utters mysteries in the Spirit" (1 Cor. 14:2).

At the same time, Paul speaks of tongues as the lowest of the gifts. And he calls his Corinthian brothers to desire the higher things: prophecy and, highest of all, charity.

(Implicit in Paul's treatment here is the distinction between two types of grace: charismatic and sanctifying. Charismatic graces are for the sake of others [see 1 Cor. 12:7]. Sanctifying grace is for one's own salvation and growth in holiness. The Church won't grow without the former, but no one can get to heaven without the latter. Indeed, one can have charismatic grace while lacking sanctifying grace [see Mt. 7:21–23].)

That covers the "what" of tongues, but we're still left with the "why," and here Paul offers a curious explanation.

"In the law it is written," he says, "'By men of strange tongues and by the lips of foreigners will I speak to this people, and even then they will not listen to me, says the Lord.' Thus, tongues are a sign not for believers but for unbelievers, while prophecy is not for unbelievers but for believers" (1 Cor. 14:20–22).

Tongues: Sign of Covenant Curse

What does he mean when he says tongues are for *unbelievers*, while prophecy is for *believers*? Doesn't that seem backward? Shouldn't tongues be for believers, who by faith are better prepared to accept strange, ecstatic behavior? Shouldn't prophecy be a sign for unbelievers, who would be impressed by insights that could only come from God? Paul's statement only makes sense when we grasp his interpretive use of two key Old Testament texts, Deuteronomy 28:49 and Isaiah 28:11.

First, he says, "in the law it is written …" This is a reference to Deuteronomy 28:49, which announces what will come right before the final curse befalls God's disobedient people. "The LORD will bring a nation against you from afar … a nation whose language you do not understand." In short, strange tongues immediately precede exile. God says, in effect: Keep my covenant, and you'll have truth; break my covenant, and you'll have death—but on the way you'll have what sounds like gibberish. Tongue-speaking in Deuteronomy 28 is a preparation for judgment, a purification, one last chance for repentance. And that's what St. Paul is talking about when he cites the passage.

The Tip of the Tongues

Second, Paul's reference to the law is indirect; he's actually quoting Isaiah 28:11: "By men of strange lips and with an alien tongue the LORD will speak to this people." What is Paul doing? Apparently, he wants his Corinthian readers to discern parallels between Isaiah's time and their own. Isaiah announced the destruction of the Northern Kingdom, immediately preceded by the ominous sign of "alien tongues." All of this would come to pass within forty years of his prophecy—when God sent final judgment in the form of the Assyrians, the most feared terrorists of the eighth century BC.

Why would God send such a judgment? Isaiah goes on to say: "The priest and the prophet reel with strong drink, they are confused with wine … they err in vision, they stumble in giving judgment" (Is. 28:7).

What are God's people to do? The priests and prophets are so drunk and demoralized that they won't proclaim the truth. Isaiah asks, "Whom will He teach knowledge, and to whom will He explain the message?" (Is. 28:9).

Does this begin to sound like the twelve tribes back in the time of Moses? Does this begin to sound like Paul's fellow Jews in first-century Corinth (see Acts 18:1–17)?

As Paul undoubtedly knew, this is what Isaiah foresaw—not just the fall of the North in the eighth century BC, but the fall of the Southern Kingdom of Judah in the distant future. And this is what Paul and all believers of the first century were living through.

Sealed with a Curse

Significantly, a portion of Isaiah's oracle is impossible to translate—and it's the verse that immediately precedes the one Paul quoted. Despite many attempts to render the original Hebrew of Isaiah 28:10 into English, Hebrew-language experts generally agree that Isaiah's words here were probably not even intelligible to the ancient prophet. Nor, apparently, were they meant to be.

This is how the passage is rendered in my Ignatius Bible: "precept upon precept, precept upon precept, line upon line, line upon line, here a little, there a little" (Is. 28:10).

Yet those words do not appear in the Hebrew.

In Hebrew, the words are: "*saw lasaw saw lasaw, qaw laqaw qaw laqaw, ze'er sham ze'er sham.*" Many commentators hold that this is nonsense poetry, childish babble. It's not meaningful Hebrew. But it needs to be explained if we're to understand what Paul says about tongue-speaking.

"By men of strange lips and with an alien tongue the LORD will speak to this people" (Is. 28:11). The Lord is preparing the people of Isaiah's time for massive judgment. They're about to be sent into exile, invaded, cut to ribbons—all because they wouldn't listen to the prophets, they wouldn't keep the Law and the covenant.

That's God's wrath. His Law is our fulfillment. The covenant curses come as fatherly discipline when we reject His love. He respects our choice, even allowing us to make hell for ourselves. If we reject His Word, then we will end up in chaos and confusion—and finally exile.

Doom came for the Northern Kingdom of Israel within a generation, at the hands of the Assyrians in 722 BC.

Extraordinary Time

The situation of the apostolic Church was little different. The powers of Jerusalem and Rome had conspired to crucify the Son of God. The people of the old covenant were in disarray. And the Romans' destruction of Jerusalem was imminent. The siege of Jerusalem in AD 70 would leave the spiritual capital of the Jews in rubble.

God sent His Spirit in power to prepare a people for living amid confusion. He sent a new Pentecost for the first generation of believers, and St. Paul was one of many Christians who received the gifts poured out upon the Church.

No wonder Paul considered tongues "a sign for unbelievers," since the gift left him not with warm, fuzzy feelings, but with a dreadful recollection of the curses of Deuteronomy 28 and the humiliating destruction of Israel by the Assyrians.

The blessings of a Pentecost, you see, are not inconsistent with times of rebellion, confusion, and judgment; indeed, such extraordinary supernatural gifts often precede times of extraordinary covenant judgment.

In from the Outside

Still, the gifts are extraordinary—by definition, they're not normal—and so they don't look right to conventional believers. Even on the first Christian Pentecost, the spectacle of the apostles speaking in tongues didn't seem to jibe with religious tradition. "And all were amazed and perplexed, saying to one another, 'What does this mean?' But others mocking said, 'They are filled with new wine'" (Acts 2:12–13).

Our own time is no different. Today, we hear critics, good people and orthodox, saying that the pentecostal experience "doesn't look Catholic." They wonder whether it might signal a lapse into Protestantism.

A bit of history is in order.

Spirited Away

The late 19th century was a time of declining belief worldwide. Modernism and biblical criticism were on the rise, obscuring the person of Jesus and making the truths of faith seem ever more elusive to believers, most especially in mainline Protestant denominations. Secularization had overtaken many traditionally Christian institutions in the West. Pope Leo XIII is said to have received a vision of

Satan's influence behind all this, and of the great struggle to come in the 20th century.

Into Pope Leo's life, in 1897, came the letters of an Italian nun, Blessed Elena Guerra, the founder of the Oblates of the Holy Spirit. She wanted the Holy Father to launch the coming century by chanting the *Veni, Creator Spiritus* ("Come, Creator Spirit") and to ask the bishops of the world to make a novena to the Holy Spirit for the renewal of the Church. The Pope would comply with her wishes, even to writing an encyclical on the Holy Spirit that very year.

Then something amazing happened. Pentecostalism emerged, seemingly out of nowhere, and began to spread rapidly. But it happened in all the "wrong" places. In Kansas, on Dec. 31, 1900, a former Methodist pastor named Charles Parham led a group in prayer for the gift of tongues, which they manifested after midnight.

At almost the same time, across the Atlantic, the Pope was fulfilling Blessed Elena's wish by chanting the *Veni, Creator Spiritus.* In short order, the pentecostal movement spread among Protestants in the United States, Central and South America, Europe, Russia, Korea, and India.

Not in Our Backyard

No wonder many Catholics see this as a Protestant phenomenon, because it started and spread outside the boundaries of the institutional Church. What many Catholics don't realize, however, is that mainline Protestantism did not recognize pentecostalism as its own, and the movement experienced its sensational growth beyond the boundaries of institutional Protestantism as well.

Still, it certainly didn't "look Catholic," and no one, to my knowledge, made a connection between Pope Leo's prayer and the emergence of pentecostalism until much later in the twentieth century. Yet Pope Leo's prayer continued to echo within the Church. In the 1950s, a Spanish priest, St. Josemaria Escriva wrote: "Ask with me for a new Pentecost, which will once again set the world alight" (*Furrow*, no. 213). And Pope John XXIII gave the prayer its most famous expression as he prepared for the Second Vatican Council.

It was in the wake of that council that, in 1967, a group of students and faculty from Duquesne University in Pittsburgh prayed for the pentecostal experience in the Catholic Church, receiving the gifts of tongues and prophecy. From Pittsburgh the movement spread to the ends of the earth. And that is a remarkable thing: from 1900 through 1967, pentecostalism was nowhere in Catholicism; yet from 1967 to the present day, you can find it almost everywhere you find Catholicism. This is not to say that everything that looks Pentecostal is supernatural. Much of it is arguably not. In some cases, it's mere emotionalism; in others, it may be fraud (or even worse). But I would hesitate to reject all of it entirely. And if any of it is genuine, then it is most certainly significant.

Northern Exposure

The question remains, then, whether this phenomenon is legitimately Catholic. Why, after all, is it entering the Church only now? I believe the answer lies in the scriptural Pentecosts. Recall that St. Paul, in speaking of tongues, refers to Deuteronomy 28, the text that predicts the curses to come when Israel violates the covenant. We see the application of those curses, not only in the first century, after Jesus' execution, but also in the eighth century BC in Isaiah's prophecy about the coming invasion of the Assyrians.

We should note that Isaiah's prophecy was directed not toward Jerusalem—that is, *not* toward the legitimate center of the covenant liturgy—but rather toward Ephraim, up north. Why would the schismatic rebels of the Northern Kingdom be first to receive extraordinary signs and judgments?

Consider the history of the North's rebellion. In 930 BC, Solomon died, and his son Rehoboam took over. Rehoboam alienated the ten tribal leaders of the northern coalition, so they rebelled. Yet God sent these Old Testament "Protestants" wave upon wave of prophets, including such greats as Elijah, Elisha, Hosea, Amos, Jonah, and Isaiah. He also sent great miracles, including the raising of the dead. (During this period, the south had no prophecy and certainly no resurrections.) Yet the north said it would have nothing to do with the house of David. And from 930 till the north's destruction in 722, the Northern Kingdom set itself apart from the rule of David's line, and also from the true worship of Jerusalem's Temple.

The people of the north were, in many ways, like Protestantism: they could point to abusive practices in government; they could point to moral corruption in the hierarchy. Yet the prophet whom the Lord sent to confront Jeroboam and the northern tribes said that it was not their unwillingness to submit to the political power of the

Davidic monarchy that provoked God. What provoked God was their rejection of the Jerusalem Temple and the liturgy established there by divine covenant. At that point, they had gone too far (see 1 Kings 13:1–34).

Yet the charism of prophecy came first to the north, as did the gift of tongues. And the Jews down south could understandably have said: "These guys can't be real Israelites. They don't sound like Israelites. And even if they are, they're worshiping in the wrong way and in the wrong place." Pentecostal phenomena, then as always, didn't fit neatly into anybody's categories.

Divine Triage

I propose that God was practicing a providential triage. Just as doctors identify the sickest patients for the most immediate care, God identified the most spiritually sickly part of His people and offered them, first, the covenantal means of restoring health. When they exhausted His efforts, He turned His healing judgment toward the south. It was then Judah's turn to receive prophecies, from the likes of Jeremiah, Ezekiel, and Joel.

As with Israel and Judah, so with the Church. Just because these strange pentecostal signs originated in Protestantism doesn't necessarily mean the signs are alien to Catholic faith. If you look through the lens of the covenant to see how the Father judges His wayward people, you'll notice that prophecy and tongues are signs He sends *first* to those who are in rebellion. *Later*, when rebellion enters the covenant people, He applies His medicine to the household as well.

How Much Does Pentecost?

Why are these signs entering the Church today? Perhaps the situation inside is becoming similar to the situation outside. What we see now in the Church—dissent, disobedience, and defections—follows upon the institutional and doctrinal dissolution of all the Protestant denominations.

As bad as Catholics have had it, Protestants have faced a *much* deeper crisis. Indeed, Catholics might not realize that the recent "revival" in what we call "Protestantism" (that is, pentecostalism and fundamentalism) is not recognized as such by traditional mainline Protestants.

What, then, is the purpose of the new Pentecost?

The Holy Spirit, it seems to me, is bringing a dramatic judgment upon a proud, stubborn, and flabby West. At the same time, through the covenant charisms that mark out God's disciplines, the Church is being propelled outward to reach cultures—in Africa and Asia—that the West had hardly bothered to reach before.

This, I believe, is the new Pentecost. God is doing a new thing, and it's what He wanted to do all the time. Only now He's doing it in spite of our sin and through His mercy. It remains for us to repent.

Christ in Majesty, Scary Jesus

A colossal mosaic, "Christ in Majesty," dominates the great upper church at the Basilica Shrine of the Immaculate Conception in Washington, DC. It is a fierce portrayal of Jesus, His passion restrained only by the fixity of the Byzantine style.

It's an image that resonates with me on many levels. Through my earliest years as a Christian—through my teens, through college, and through seminary preparation for Presbyterian ministry—my formation was overwhelmingly Calvinist, a Protestant tradition that emphasizes God's sovereignty and His judgment. "For the LORD is our judge, the LORD is our ruler, the LORD is our king," said the prophet Isaiah (Is. 33:22). And that's how Jesus appears in the Basilica. The irony is that my Calvinist background prepared me to think of Christ that way, but not to *see* Him that way—at least not in this life. The reformer John Calvin was a forceful opponent of devotional images, favoring bare church walls and even bare crosses. He held that images—even images of Christ—presented a temptation to idolatry, the worship of a temporal sign in place of the sovereign and transcendent Lord.

I am now two decades a Roman Catholic. Yet every time I kneel beneath that overpowering image I wonder whether it is my vestigial inner Calvinist that thrills at what

I see—thrilling, nevertheless, as only a Catholic can thrill before a sacred image.

Some years ago, an essayist nicknamed this icon "Scary Jesus."[1] And it does seem to violate the canons of the Christian greeting-card industry. Contemporary Christian art bids us imagine the Lord backing up the goalie in a junior-varsity soccer game, or hugging teens on prom night. In the modern icon, Jesus is the nice guy Norman Rockwell somehow missed in all those Saturday Evening Post covers. "Scary Jesus" doesn't fit the profile.

Still, there is a more disquieting paradox at work in "Christ in Majesty." The mosaic portrays Christ in judgment, as we might encounter Him in the Book of Revelation. But doesn't the same book portray Christ as a lamb, so gentle that He can pass for dead (Rev. 5:6)? Didn't the Word become flesh as a man who blessed the meek and didn't fight back?

The icon forces us to confront a seeming contradiction in Christianity: our Lord is a just judge, a powerful vindi-cator, whose wrath is capable of consigning mortal sinners to hell; yet our Lord is merciful and as meek as a lowly barnyard animal in its infancy.

Some people have tried to reconcile these images by making them sequential. Jesus was soft and tender in His first coming, they say, but with the second coming the gloves will be off, and then it's no more Mr. Nice Guy. Well, this doesn't work—first, because the Gospels show us that Jesus did indeed vent His wrath on wicked men during His earthly life (e.g., Mt. 15:3–9; 21:12–13;

---

[1] Paul C. Fox, "Facing the Scary Jesus," *New Covenant*, April 2000, 30–31.

23:13–16); but also because the Book of Revelation shows our Lord to be a Lamb to the very end, at the consummation of all human history (Rev. 21:22, 22:3).

So which shall we worship? Which shall we contemplate? The Judge or the Lamb? Scary Jesus or Mr. Nice Guy? Which is the true Lord and Christ?

The dogmatic truth is that we need not choose. The mystery of the Incarnation demands that we accept the perfect union of many seemingly incompatible things: the finite contains the infinite; the eternal enters time; the sacrificial lamb presides on the Day of Wrath (Rev. 6:15–17; 14:9–10).

This is not a subtlety reserved for theologians. Dock workers and poultry keepers, washer women and seamstresses have known this since the birthday of the Church. Even those who could not read knew the truth of Christ because of icons like "Christ in Majesty."

In the eighth century a movement arose in the eastern churches to do away with sacred images. It was a movement of elites—intellectuals, theologians, and emperors. They thought that icons were an insult to God's glory and majesty, which cannot really be portrayed. The transcendent God should be worshipped only with the intellect, they said. They received an imperial license to destroy the icons in the churches; and for this they earned the name "iconoclasts," image-smashers.

The saints, however, opposed these elites and the saints prevailed. They called themselves "iconodules," or those who honor icons. And they argued that since God had condescended to take on flesh, the common people had the right to contemplate Him enfleshed. The most eloquent of the iconodules, St. Theodore of Studion, wrote that Christ "does not abandon the exalted reality of his divinity, which is immaterial and cannot be circumscribed; and yet it is his glory to abase himself in such a noble manner down to our own level that now in his body he can be circumscribed. he has become matter, that is, flesh, he who sustains everything that exists; and he is not ashamed to have become what he has taken on, and to be called such."[2]

The truth is that the iconoclasts despised the humility of God. He had scandalized them by assuming human flesh, by bleeding and dying, and they wanted Him safely back in His heaven.

But that cannot be because the Word was made flesh and dwelt among us—and He still has that flesh. He didn't shed it the way a snake sheds its skin. He glorified that flesh and now offers it as love to the Father. What the face of the human Jesus revealed in the first century, the icon reveals in the eighth and the twenty-first centuries. Even when the icon portrays "Christ in Majesty," it also portrays Christ's humility. For we see as through a glass darkly, and our idea of glory is a far cry from heavenly, but God has accommodated Himself to our vision. What is scandalous about the icon is simply the scandal of the Incarnation, with all its paradoxes.

From the last supper onward, Christ has magnified the scandal. For the Word who became flesh willed that we should encounter His flesh in the appearance of bread, in the Eucharist. Veiled from our view is His Resurrection

---

[2] Quoted in Christoph von Schönborn, *God's Human Face: The Christ-icon*, trans. Lothar Kraugh (San Francisco: Ignatius, 1994), 234.

glory, His divinized humanity, and yet He won't have any more glory when He returns at the end of time. The only difference will be that, in the end, "we shall see him as he is" (1 Jn. 3:2). We shall see His glory.

There's a sense in which we already see Him "as he is" in the Eucharist. The reality of Jesus is conveyed by the appearance of bread. He hasn't ceased to be humble and He'll never cease to show mercy—except to those who freely reject His mercy, with a freedom He respects for all eternity.

In the Eucharist, Christ appears as precisely the king He promised to be. At the last supper He told His disciples, "The kings of the Gentiles exercise lordship over them. . . . I am among you as one who serves. . . . that you may eat and drink at my table in my kingdom" (Lk. 22:25, 27, 30). The kingdom of Jesus Christ will never cease to be exercised primarily in terms of love that is life-giving. Yet His power is of a different order than the world's idea of power, and the wrath of the Lamb differs significantly from human vengeance.

When we stand in the presence of Christ, we know ourselves to be judged, because we see ourselves simultaneously in the light of perfect majesty and perfect humility. If we profess the real presence of Christ in the Eucharist, our pride should wither when we go to Mass.

In the Mass, "Christ our Paschal Lamb has been sacrificed" (1 Cor. 5:7), and St. Paul emphasizes that this brings us into judgment: "Whoever, therefore, eats the bread or drinks the cup of the Lord in an unworthy manner will be guilty of profaning the body and blood of the Lord. . . . For any one who eats and drinks without discerning the body eats and drinks judgment upon himself" (1 Cor. 11:27, 29).

Nevertheless, Jesus bade us repeatedly to come forward: "I am the bread of life; he who comes to me shall not hunger, and he who believes in me shall never thirst. . . . [H]e who eats my flesh and drinks my blood has eternal life, and I will raise him up at the last day" (Jn. 6:35, 54).

This is the Christ I see in the majestic mosaic, the Christ I receive in the Eucharist—my sovereign Lord, who has become a lamb, who gives Himself as bread.

Chapter Nine

"My Words Are Spirit and Life":
Teachings from the Scriptural and Eucharistic Heart of Jesus

I am only now beginning to know and appreciate my heritage in the Church of Pittsburgh. When I grew up in the South Hills, my family was Presbyterian, and it made a difference. My Catholic friends had their own way of marking geography. It was as if they could see an additional dimension that was invisible to me. Where I saw clear borders between boroughs and school districts, they saw even clearer parish boundaries. It wasn't so much whether you were from Bethel or Upper St. Clair as whether you were from St. Val's, St. Germaine's, St. Bernard's, or St. Louise's.

And these kids knew the names of pastors—Father Lonergan, Father Hugo—the way I knew the names of the Pirates: Bill Mazeroski, Willie Stargell, Manny Sanguillen, Roberto Clemente.

Back then I dreamt of being able to hit like Clemente but I found a better way to imitate him. In 1985 I was received into full communion with the Catholic Church, as Roberto Clemente had been, decades before as a teenager in Puerto Rico.

Delivered as the keynote address at the Total Catholic Education Conference, sponsored by the Diocese of Pittsburgh, October 22, 2005. The text has been adapted and updated slightly.

So … though I am a native of Pittsburgh, I am a relative newcomer to its Church—a Church that has deep, deep roots, and a long and rich history. I am just now learning about the men and women who laid the foundations of this diocese—men and women who poured the concrete for its schools, and men and women who taught in its classrooms. As much as they poured foundation, they poured themselves out—they gave themselves entirely—so that we might live faithful lives here today.

That is the legacy they've left us. That is the legacy we must pass on, as teachers of the faith. We must pour ourselves out; give ourselves entirely, for the sake of the people we teach. We must pass on what we've been given, and we must light a fire in the hearts of the next generation, so that, when their day comes, they'll do the same.

With that in mind, I have to say that whoever came up with the theme for this Conference must have been divinely inspired. "From his Heart … Rivers of Living Water"—those few words draw our attention to the Sacred Heart of Jesus. And that's the ultimate point of our Catholic genealogy. The Sacred Heart of Jesus is the source of the rivers of living water that run through Catholic history, rivers mightier than the three rivers that define this city. The Sacred Heart of Jesus is the source of the rivers of living water that run through us to our students, when we teach with fidelity, as our ancestors did.

We must go to that source, and go often, if we want to persevere and succeed as teachers of the faith. For we cannot give away what we do not first possess. And we will quickly run out, dry out, burn out, as teachers, unless we possess that living water in abundance.

Jesus said: "He who believes in me, as the scripture has said, 'Out of his heart shall flow rivers of living water'" (Jn. 7:38). And John goes on to tell us: "Now this he said about the Spirit, which those who believed in him were to receive" (Jn. 7:39).

John is a great literary artist. He does not place such a dramatic line early in his Gospel unless he is going to bring it to fulfillment later. If he portrays Jesus promising the Spirit in chapter 7, you better believe that Jesus will deliver the Spirit by chapter 20. And so he does.

As Jesus' three hours on the cross drew to a close, He took a sip of the wine that was offered to Him on a sponge. And then "he said, 'It is finished'; and he bowed his head and gave up his spirit" (Jn. 19:30).

How did that action—the handing over of His Spirit—manifest itself to the onlookers?

"One of the soldiers pierced his side with a spear, and at once there came out blood and water" (Jn. 19:34).

Very few passages of the Bible have so captured the attention, the imagination, and the fervor of the Church and her saints as these passages. And that shouldn't surprise us. As I said just a moment ago, John the Evangelist was a great literary artist. And this moment was the narrative climax of his drama.

Today I would like to focus on two classic interpretations of that text. The first we find in the Fathers of the Church and surely reflects the original intention of St. John. That first interpretation presents the scene as a giving of the sacraments: the blood representing the Eucharist and the water representing baptism. The second classic interpretation is best expressed by St. Thomas Aquinas, who saw the heart of Christ as a mystical and allegorical representation of the Scriptures, which were opened up to us by the giving of Christ's Spirit, the shedding of Christ's blood, the rending of the veil.

The open heart of Christ is the source of the sacraments.

The open heart of Christ is the very Spirit and image of the Scriptures.

These two complementary interpretations, I believe, are our keys to effective teaching. They are the antidote to burnout. They provide us with unlimited access to that living water that flows from the heart of Christ, and must flow from our hearts, too, in our teaching.

The Sacramental Reading

The sacramental reading of John 19:34 was the common property of the Fathers of the Church. But it was not their invention. The sacramental reading is not a pious allegory imposed by later Christians upon an unsuspecting primitive text.

No. In interpreting John in this way, the Church Fathers were merely *reflecting faithfully upon the earliest Christian witness*. For the sacramental reading was the original intention of the author of the Gospel. And, more than that, it was the original intention of Jesus.

Again, this is not a pious fantasy. It is a verdict upheld by many modern biblical scholars, both Protestant and Catholic. No less a critical scholar than Father Raymond Brown has upheld the sacramental reading after exhaustive study. In his last, posthumously published study of John's Gospel, Father Brown wrote: "in a dramatic scene, John shows symbolically that both of these sacraments, baptismal water and eucharistic blood, have the source of their existence and power in the death of Jesus." John shows "the sacramental undertones of the words and works of Jesus that were already part of the Gospel tradition."[1]

John meant it. Jesus meant it. And it is a core truth of the Gospel. Jesus came to give us the Spirit. He came to give us the sacraments as the ordinary means of receiving the Spirit. The giving is a single action, a single outpouring from the heart of God. But it takes place in us over the course of a lifetime—begun in Baptism, completed in Confirmation, and renewed in every Confession and Communion.

The sacraments are our strength. As teachers of the Catholic faith, we are strong not just in our own school spirit, but in the eternal Spirit, who is invincible and all-powerful. By the grace of the sacraments, our students, too, are strong in the Spirit, and it is imperative that we help them to face up to that reality.

That's our work. It's a work of *mystagogy*, like the opening of Jesus' heart upon the cross. We guide students into the mystery of Christ, into the mysteries of Christ, and we help them to make their dwelling there.

The Biblical Reading

Thomas Aquinas saw the open heart of Jesus from a different angle. His view complements the sacramental view, which he also upheld. "By 'the heart' of Christ," Thomas wrote, "one understands Sacred Scripture, which manifests

---

[1] Raymond E. Brown, *An Introduction to the Gospel of John* (New York: Doubleday, 2003), 234.

the heart of Christ. For this [heart] was closed before the passion, because [Scripture] was obscure; but [Scripture] is open after the passion, because the [disciples] now read it with understanding and see how the prophets are to be interpreted."[2]

When Jesus' heart was pierced, the veil of the Temple was torn in two, and the mysterious plan of God was revealed once and for all. St. Paul, who loved the Old Testament, explained to the Corinthians that, until Christ's saving death, a veil lay over the Scriptures. Jesus' death removed the veil forever, and His sacramental graces continue, even today, to remove the veil for each and every one of us. "When a man turns to the Lord," said St. Paul, "the veil is removed" (2 Cor. 3:16).

We turn to the Lord, really present, especially when we encounter His holy Scriptures in the Mass. For the Mass is the only thing Catholics are required to do every week. And the Bible is the only book that has to be read in every Mass.

The opening of Jesus' Sacred Heart has made it possible for us to read the Bible and hear the Bible—both testaments of the Bible—with an understanding of God's overarching plan, and our own part in that plan, and the destiny of our souls and of all creation. The opening of Jesus' heart is the very meaning of divine revelation. God has revealed Himself to us in a way that is profound and personal and communal. It is scriptural, and so it is Catholic.

---

[2] St. Thomas Aquinas, *Commentary on the Psalms*, no. 21.

My colleague Michael Waldstein once wrote: "In all its diversity, Scripture does one thing. It manifests the heart of Christ. The heart of Christ, in turn, makes the Scriptures intelligible, because it is only through [the heart of Christ] that the disciples understand the Scriptures."[3]

And so that's where we disciples go: to the heart of Christ, the heart of the Scriptures.

The Two Tables

I said earlier that these two actions we discern in John 19:34—the giving of the sacraments and the opening of the Scriptures—were but a single action of Christ on the cross. Perhaps they are two rivers of living water, but they flow from that single source, which is the heart of Christ.

They remain, even today, a single action in history. For they constitute the two movements, as it were, of the Mass: the Liturgy of the Word and the Liturgy of the Eucharist.

The Second Vatican Council shifted the metaphor but delivered the same message, as it urged us to nourish ourselves from the two tables of the sacred liturgy: "the table of the Lord's body" (*Dei Verbum* 48) and "the table of God's word" (*Dei Verbum* 51).

What is it that happens at the Mass? The same thing that the two disciples experienced on the road to Emmaus and in the supper at their destination. Jesus interpreted the Scriptures to them as they walked along the road at dusk. Then they *knew Him* in the breaking of the bread. What

---

[3] Michael M. Waldstein, "On Scripture in the Summa Theologiae," *The Aquinas Review*, I (1994), 77.

do we see there, but the Liturgy of the Word, and then the Liturgy of the Eucharist?

We read that the disciples' hearts burned within them as they walked along with Jesus, as they sat at table with Him. And then He vanished from their sight.

What a curious thing! If Jesus had been out to prove something, He could have performed great miracles, appearing in glory in the sky above Jerusalem for tens of thousands of people to see.

But He didn't do that. Instead, He walked with two disciples, interpreted the Scriptures for them, led them to His Eucharistic presence, and then left them with burning hearts.

What more could we, as teachers, hope to do?

St. Augustine once said that the teaching of the faith was not so much lecturing and preparing lesson plans as "one heart setting another on fire."

"One heart setting another on fire." That's what we're doing, as teachers, as catechists, as administrators, as preachers, as volunteers, as parents. We're not drones and drudges, slaves to the system, or whatever other terms we might prefer to express dissatisfaction in a job. Because we're not doing a job. We've come to cast a fire upon the earth, and would that it were already kindled!

Our God made us this way because He made us in His image and then perfected us in His image in Jesus Christ.

Where does He set our hearts on fire today? In the Mass, where He opens up His heart. In the Mass, where He opens up the Scriptures.

That's where we're most perfectly conformed to the image of God. That's where we become one, in the closest communion, with the eternal Son of God. We live His life—all of it. We burn with His fire. Afterward, we open our hearts, wherever we go, to give living water to the people, all around us, who are thirsting with a thirst as big as almighty God—a thirst that only God can quench.

We even suffer to make it happen. St. Paul said he *rejoiced* to suffer for the sake of his teaching of the faith. "Now I *rejoice* in my sufferings for your sake, and in my flesh I complete what is lacking in Christ's afflictions for the sake of his body, that is, the church" (Col. 1:24, emphasis added).

Don't get me wrong. I don't mean to glorify suffering or promote a bloody cult of a blind god who would pummel his son mercilessly as a substitute for the sinful world.

No, that's not the Catholic faith. That's not how we understand our redemption. Jesus suffered mightily to open up the Scriptures for us and give us the sacraments. But pain is not what endowed Christ's suffering and death with its infinite value and power. It wasn't so much His pain as His love—His love for which He would endure any amount of pain and hardship.

Love is what endowed Christ's suffering and death with its infinite value and power. Opponents of Christianity sometimes claim that other people have suffered more than Jesus. Maybe, maybe not. But one thing's for sure: no one has ever loved more. And nowhere is Jesus' love more active than in His obedience unto death.

Son though He was, master though He was, teacher though He was, Jesus "emptied himself, taking the form of a servant, being born in the likeness of men. And being found in human form he humbled himself and became obedient unto death, even death on a cross" (Phil. 2:7–8).

As teachers, catechists, and parents—as Christians—we need to learn from the example of this God who emptied Himself, blood and water, upon the cross of His self-offering. We need to be His disciples first, to receive His life as our own, before we can pass it on. We need to receive the Word of God at His holy table, and then meditate on it deeply, weave it into our prayer and into our actions, and finally into our teaching. We need to live the life of Christ on earth today, then teach the life of Christ to the next generation.

We need to be disciples first and apostles second. We need to discipline ourselves to study with constancy before we can teach effectively. No matter how many degrees we hold, we can be sure that we have not even begun to plumb the divine mysteries. We must be learning along with our students, always feeding ourselves so that we remain strong enough to feed our children.

We must not approach the mysteries of faith as mere fodder for lesson plans. We need to let the truth sanctify us. God wants to make us saints more than He wants to use us to make others saints. And, make no mistake about it, that's what we're doing when we're teaching the faith, no matter what our venue, no matter what our methods or technology. We must be saints whom God uses to make more saints.

If you watch the evening news fairly regularly, you'll see many images of disaster. People turned out of their homes by floods and earthquakes, thirsting for sanitary drinking water, hungry for a morsel to eat. . . . My dear fellow teachers, we face no less a crisis in this land that we love. We face neighborhoods full of people thirsting for living water—and not even knowing how to slake their thirst. They demand our works of mercy every bit as much as the displaced thousands of faraway evacuees. Through the prophets God taught us to do the works of mercy, and the greater works are the spiritual: instructing the ignorant and correcting those in error.

That's our call as teachers. We need to feed so many. We need to quench so many who thirst. But we won't have the strength to do it if we're not first tending to our own spiritual needs. We cannot help others find forgiveness if we're getting to Confession sporadically. We need to go at least once a month. We cannot help others grow in Eucharistic faith if we consider missing Mass an option in our weekend plans. No way. We should even try to get to Mass more often than Sundays and holy days. Many people go daily and many more could, with a little bit of effort.

We need to go deeply into the mysteries. We need to take up serious Catholic Bible study—Bible study that does what I'm talking about today—Bible study that looks upon Scripture as the heart of Christ, opened on the cross, opened in the Mass. We need to know the revealed basis of what we believe and what we teach about the Scriptures and about the Mass. Jesus Christ is really present! Knowing it doesn't make it more real, but *not* knowing it certainly makes our sacramental experience unfruitful.

In our prayer and in our study, we need to be daring like St. Thomas the Apostle, who began the first Sacred Heart devotions in history when he placed his hands in the wounded heart of the Risen Lord. Our study of the Scripture, our sacramental life should do for us what it did for Thomas. It impelled him to cry out, "My Lord and my

God!" (Jn. 20:28)—a most sublime, concise, and incarnational creed. Then he traveled to the far ends of the earth to teach the most distant peoples about Jesus Christ. And those people, along the eastern coast of India, still refer to themselves as Thomas Christians as they pass on the faith amid persecution, as they endure in a hostile culture, as they prepare another generation to pass on what they have received.

That's love. We pour ourselves out completely. It doesn't matter whether we're lay people, priests, or consecrated sisters or brothers. Our giving must be complete.

In Pittsburgh we need only look around us to learn that lesson. Look at the domed basilica on Polish Hill. Look at the spires and the schools in so many neighborhoods. Many of them were built by steelworkers who reported for duty at the parish as soon as they finished their shift in the mill. They literally laid the foundations of our Church, of our churches. They poured themselves out as they poured the concrete, for the sake of their children—for our sake— and for Christ's sake! And that's love.

I don't mean to diminish the contributions of the bishops—from Michael O'Connor through Regis Canevin, John Wright to Donald Wuerl and David Zubik. They spent themselves without holding anything back. Nor do I mean to downplay the nuns, who staffed those schools and ran every classroom with professional excellence. Nor, once again, should I forget the priests who sanctified those local labors through the centuries. Their names will live on, in a prominent place in American Catholic history: the Servant of God Demetrius Gallitzin, St. John Neumann, Blessed Francis Xavier Seelos, Father Suitbert Mollinger, Father

James Cox, Father John Hugo. There were giants on our earth in those days.

But the sacrifice was everyone's. Not just the priests' and sisters', though thank God for the part they played. The sacrifice was everyone's, and it is ours. As teachers, we have to empty ourselves, pour out our hearts, excel all others in love, open up the Scriptures, witness to the sacraments, and make enormous sacrifices—all in imitation of our Teacher. All in imitation of Jesus. All in communion with Jesus.

Notes

LETTER & SPIRIT

Series

Letter & Spirit seeks to foster a deeper conversation about the Bible. This new journal of biblical theology, published in collaboration with Scott Hahn and the St. Paul Center for Biblical Theology, takes a crucial step toward recovering the fundamental link between the literary and historical study of Scripture and its religious and spiritual meaning in the Church's liturgy and Tradition.

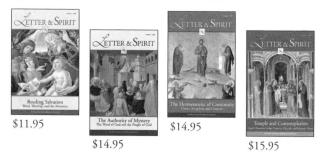

$11.95

$14.95

$14.95

$15.95

Letter & Spirit, Vol. I: Reading Salvation
Word, Worship, and the Mysteries
This inaugural issue captures something of the enormity of what the Church claims for Scripture. To read Scripture is to be "reading salvation." Here we encounter the living Word of God who desires to lead all humankind to worship and communion in the mystery of His own divine life.

Letter & Spirit, Vol. II: The Authority of Mystery
The Word of God and the People of God
The Authority of Mystery brings together great minds of the past and present to consider the relationship between the Word of God and the people of God, the Church.

Letter & Spirit, Vol. III: The Hermeneutic of Continuity
Christ, Kindom, and Creation
This volume features important contributions from Pope Benedict XVI, Cardinal Christoph Schonborn, and Cardinal Avery Dulles.

Letter & Spirit, Vol. IV: Temple and Contemplation
God's Presence in the Cosmos, Church, and Human Heart
Inspired by the ground-breaking work of Yves Congar and Jean Danielou, this volume includes contributions on such topics as the Tabernacle and the origins of Christian mysticism; Jesus self-consciousness of being the new Temple and the new High Priest; and the doctrine of the indwelling of the Trinity in the soul.

(800) 398-5470
Visit us on the Web for more books by outstanding Catholic authors!
www.emmausroad.org